A Rainbow Book

Praise for *The Best You Can Do—*

"This is a very helpful little book for children of aging parents.

"Most people fortunate enough to have elderly parents and to have the opportunity to be involved in their care will face a number of major and often difficult issues. This book goes through the major issues involved with an older person's increasing care needs, describes how children react and learn to cope, and gives useful advice on how to address these issues. It starts with advice on how to offer limited assistance and progresses though home care considerations all the way to dealing with the possibility of needing to move a parent into an institutional setting.

"It is a practical book with many positive and useful suggestions for facing these issues successfully, while minimizing stress and guilt. It comes from the perspective of an experienced counselor and leader of many support groups."

—Laurence Z. Rubenstein, MD, MPH, FACP,
Professor and Chairman,
Reynolds Department of Geriatric Medicine,
The University of Oklahoma, HSC

"Day-to-day caregiving is about identifying concerns and implementing solutions—all while your focus has to stay true to the love you have for your care receiver. *The Best You Can Do* helps you work through these every day challenges to keep your life and sanity intact!"

—Joni Aldrich, author, speaker
and radio show host of *Caregiving SOS*

"Here's relief for those whose time and energies are consumed by responsibility for an aging relative. In a personal, storytelling style this little book offers a step-by-step approach to self-understanding and permission to regain balance in their lives.

"I myself am now an aging parent, and I still rely on some of the insights and skills I gained in Carol Pierskalla's first seminar."

—Jane Dewey Heald, seminar participant, support group leader, and coauthor of *Help for Families of the Aging*

"Many books are now available for patients and caregivers facing those final years with Alzheimer's disease or the frailties that come after a life full of years. A number of additional books are available to help families deal with end-of-life decisions. This is a workbook for those who seek self-help.

"The focus of Dr. Pierskalla's teachings is directed to the caregiver, and in case after case it is the adult child, usually a daughter, of a parent who has come to his or her final decline. If the reader has the capacity for introspection, then this will be a very useful book. It will add to your insight.

"Starting with the premise that there are opportunities to know thyself better, the author shares many stories that border on parable. Each example offers up an opportunity to critically look at the situation and work toward an understanding that benefits all parties. This is an exercise in listening and in compromise. It is not goal oriented to problem solving.

"I particularly enjoyed one of the phrases in Chapter 9. In discussing how change should be incremental she notes that 'burning our bridges is not a good idea.' There is also an entire section devoted to asking good questions and another section that gives one an opportunity for self-affirmation.

"I recommend this book to those family caregivers who can roll up their sleeves, address the situation with their parents and siblings objectively, and make changes in their own lives as they impact the lives of those around them."

—Eric G. Tangalos, MD, FACP, AGSF, CMD, Professor of Medicine and Chair, Emeritus, Primary Care Internal Medicine, Mayo Clinic

The Best You Can Do

For Yourself and Your Aging Parent

CAROL SPARGO PIERSKALLA, PH.D.

Rainbow Books, Inc.
FLORIDA

The Best You Can Do: For Yourself and Your Aging Parent
© 2013 by Carol Spargo Pierskalla, Ph.D.

Softcover ISBN 978-1-56825-155-4
ePub (ebook) ISBN 978-1-56825-156-1

Published by

Rainbow Books, Inc.
P. O. Box 430 Highland City, FL 33846-0430

Editorial Offices and Wholesale/Distributor Orders

Telephone: (863) 648-4420
RBIbooks@aol.com
RainbowBooksInc.com

Author's Website

CarolPierskalla.com

Individuals' Orders

Toll-free Telephone (800) 431-1579
Amazon.com
AllBookStores.com
BookCH.com

Photos by Image Photography, Bemidji, Minnesota.

Disclaimer: This book is not intended to serve as a substitute for legal or psychological advice or counsel. Each individual situation is different, and the reader is encouraged to seek legal or psychological counsel regarding any specific questions.

The paper used in this publication meets the minimum requirements of the American National Standard for Information Sciences—Permanence of Paper for Printed Library Materials, ANSI Z39.48-1984.

First Edition 2013
17 16 15 14 13   7 6 5 4 3 2 1
Produced and printed in the United States of America.

To caregivers past, present and future —
and in particular to

Chris De La Cruz
Jim Spargo
Bill Pierskalla
Jane Heald

Contents

Other Books by Carol Spargo Pierskalla, Ph.D. —

Help for Families of the Aging: A Small-Group Seminar by Carol
Spargo Pierskalla and Jane Dewey Heald

*Help for Families of the Aging: Caregivers Can Express Love and
Set Limits: A Seminar Leader's Manual* by Carol Spargo Pierskalla
(1983)

Help for Families of the Aging: Seminar Workbook by Carol Spargo
Pierskalla and Dewey Jane Heald (1988)

Miles Ahead: Devotions from Older Adults edited by Carol Spargo
Pierskalla (2001, includes three of Dr. Pierskalla's original parables:
"The River's Run," "The Hedgerow" and "The Perfect Pot")

Rehearsal for Retirement: My Journey into the Future by Carol
Spargo Pierskalla (1991)

Rehearsal for Retirement by Carol Spargo Pierskalla and National
Ministries (1992)

Introduction

We call them the "umbrella" generation, that generation above us that stands sentinel, shielding us from the uncertainties of life.

But the parental umbrella collapsed, trapping us in a downpour of heart attack, stroke, cancer, broken bones, arthritis, pneumonia and/or dementia.

The book you hold in your hands is your way out of the storm, back into a gentler breeze, a quiet drizzle. It's not sunlight; it's not a thundering gale either.

I can't promise you good enough weather for a day at the beach, but I can tell this: you are not alone.

My purpose in writing this book is to share the liberation that I have seen caregivers experience when they worked through the assumptions about what they "ought" to be doing. I'm giving you permission to re-think cultural and family expectations, which sometimes do not fit with twenty-first century life styles.

My husband and I have been caregivers for our four parents, and I have also led many caregiver seminars and authored/co-authored several books on the subject of caregiving.

The little book you hold in your hand is a distillation of the wisdom I have gained from both my own experience and from helping other caregivers. I suggest that you read the book through once, then, if possible, recruit a trusted friend to debrief you on the exercises. (Make sure your debriefing person has read Appendix C: Notes to the Listener.)

After you study this book and have the courage to complete the exercises, your attitudes will begin to change. Throughout the following pages, you will meet many other caregivers. Hopefully their stories will give you courage and faith.

My thoughts and prayers are with you,
Carol Spargo Pierskalla

Chapter 1

You Are Not Alone.

Won't somebody help me, please?

You wake up one morning and realize that life as you've known it is gone. It could have happened overnight; it could have taken months or years — but it is gone. Whatever you were before, whatever your life was, you are now a caregiver for an aging parent. Your parent's needs have changed your life and the lives of those around you in ways you never anticipated.

Joan's Journal

Meet Joan, a wife and mother who is suddenly responsible for her aging mother. Whether or not you find similarities between yourself and Joan as she pours out her heart in her journal, she will assure you of one thing: *You are not alone.*

December 1

I cannot believe it has finally happened. After saying over and over again that Mother would never live with us, we finally moved her in yesterday. It was exciting, in a way, because we do love her so. The kids were happy and glad that Grandma could be here — they love her cookies — but I know that it means a total change of lifestyle for me. Maybe it will work out okay, but I will miss my quiet morning coffee and my freedom to come and go during the day. John has promised to help and so have the kids. We'll see. Maybe it will work.

December 20

I can't believe the confusion here. There is so much to be done, but it's almost impossible to find space in my own kitchen. Mother decided to bake dozens of Christmas cookies, and I thought it was a good idea. But now I can't even find space to cook dinner. Between taking her shopping and mailing her Christmas cards — 147 of them — I haven't finished my own shopping or mailed more than half of my own cards.

Dear John took her shopping one night, and that was it for him. He came home absolutely worn out and totally frustrated. "We looked at three hundred scarves for your aunt Millie and then she bought her an umbrella."

Poor John. He's way out of his element here.

What am I talking about? As if I'm not!

January 29

Mother fell on the ice last week. Luckily she didn't break her hip, but she did sprain her ankle and has a slight concussion; she's been in rehab for a week. The house seems so peaceful. I guess I never realized how much I valued my alone time.

She's coming home tomorrow, and we've been moving her bedroom down to the study and moving the study up to her bedroom. It will be easier to get her to the bathroom, and she will be able to be more involved in what goes on if she's down here.

Of course, it means that I won't be able to get away for privacy without going upstairs. I feel so wicked when I have thoughts like that.

Why can't I love her more and myself less? I can't stand myself when I wallow around in self-pity this way — as though she's not suffering and

I am. She has no one but us now, with Dad gone. I remember how good she was to him during his illness and how lonely she was when he died.

Dear God, help me to love her so much that I never again feel put upon or inconvenienced by her.

February 14

Has it been only two weeks? I have been out of the house just once and that was to do the grocery shopping.

The kids have taken my kitchen TV upstairs to the study so they can watch their own programs.

Mother watches the soaps all day long.

I can't stand it much longer.

John says we'll have to give her a small TV for her birthday. She can have it in her room, and then I might get some peace.

When I disappear upstairs during the day, she asks me where I'm going, and I have to lie, saying, "I'm going to put away the laundry" or "I have to make the beds" — anything so she doesn't think I'm running away from her, which I am.

Lord, help me.

March 10

The TV-in-her-room idea didn't work. She says it's too lonely in her room watching it by herself. The kids are almost never downstairs anymore. John is finding excuses to stay away from home. Tomorrow I will turn off the TV and talk to her about it.

March 12

Well, I did it. I talked to her. I tried to be gentle, but I finally lost my cool a little. When I told her that the TV bothered me, she said. "Are you saying I'm a bother and a nuisance?"

"No, I'm just saying that it would be better if the TV weren't on so much. I don't like soaps, so you should watch them in your room."

"Maybe I should just leave and go back home."

"Mom, I'm not saying that. Be reasonable."

"I am being reasonable. You're the one who's being unreasonable."

Score: Mom 1, Daughter 0

So now we don't have the TV on. We have total silence, and she's been in her room ever since. I know she's sulking, but somehow that doesn't help me. I feel like a louse — a selfish louse.

What am I going to do?

March 24

Well, things are back to normal. Mom is back in the living room with the TV, but that is better than the guilt and misery I felt when she shut herself up in her room.

I really just sort of exist from day to day. I talked to Esther about the problem, but she thinks my mother is "adorable" and would like to trade hers for mine. So, she's no help. In fact, she gave me kind of a funny look when I expressed how frustrated I was. I think she was shocked.

Actually, I guess it's not so bad. I must be getting used to it. I've read so many novels that I can't believe it. I've had to give up the bridge club several times now, but that's okay too. It's my privacy I miss, not my friends.

April 23

I can't believe how things have changed over the past month. It seems like years. On April 1, Mom went out for a walk, as she usually does in the mornings when it's nice, and she got lost. We spent several hours searching for her, with help of the police and all our neighbors. She was found miles away in a strange neighborhood in a sort of daze. She was frightened and asked us where we had been and why we had moved without her.

Can you believe it? Now you can imagine what it's like . . . No more bridge clubs, no more lunches or church or anything else — unless John or one of the kids will stay here and watch her.

We replaced our gas range in the kitchen with an electric one; I was afraid she would gas us all some morning.

Oh, well. This too will pass. Is that supposed to be helpful? Sure, it will pass and something more awful will probably happen . . .

June 4

John and I took the weekend off. Just the two of us. What a luxury!

We hired someone from the Home Health Agency to come and stay for a week so we could get away. Expensive but worth it.

We found a little resort hotel and slept late and walked and talked and ate and were lazy. At first it was great fun, but then I realized that I was doing all the talking, and all I talked about was Mom and how miserable I was. Then I cried and John held me. I promised not to mention it again — but then I had nothing to say to him!

It's as though I've been in solitary confinement or something. I'm neither interested in anything else nor do I care about anything else. John tried to be helpful, but he doesn't really understand. No one does.

While we were gone, Mom had a little attack of some kind. That seems to happen every time we try to get away. I hate to see her this way. Why can't she be like her old self?

That's a dumb question!

July 1

We had to cancel our vacation plans because Mom got sick at the last minute, and we didn't feel we could leave her with the baby sitter — horrible word to use about the person who is staying with your own mother. *Will this ever end?* It seems like years — not months since she came.

Why does God allow this?

Reverend Johnson came by yesterday.

"It's such a wonderful thing you're doing," he said. "I think everyone should take care of their parents the way you are. Then we wouldn't need those awful nursing homes."

I wanted to shout at him, "What do you know? And what about when I can't do this anymore? Then will you tell me I'm doing the *wrong* thing?"

Of course, I didn't shout. I just asked him if he wanted more cookies or coffee.

For the first time, I'm beginning to understand why nursing homes are necessary.

August 4

Mother had a bathroom-type accident yesterday. What a mess and how embarrassed she was.

"I'm so sorry, I'm so sorry," she kept repeating.

I didn't know who to feel sorrier for, me or her.

The kids were horrified. So was John. So was I, for that matter.

September 5

The kids are back in school and so there's more peace here. Mom seems to have settled down too. I think she felt the tension from me as I tried to do all the things the kids wanted to do all summer and still make sure that she wasn't left alone. Yesterday we had our first good talk in a long time.

"Remember the trip we took to Alaska in that old Nash Rambler?" she asked.

"Yeah. I remember the leaky tent, too. I remember you putting your shower cap on so the leaks didn't mess up your hair during the night."

We laughed together. It was really pleasant.

"It would be fun to do that again," she said.

"Wouldn't it!" I agreed, and we smiled at each other.

Then she looked around and said, "Where is your father keeping himself these days?"

That really blew my mind. But it's okay. At least for a while it felt like she was my old mommy again. I wish it could be like that more often. Later I walked around crying for two hours. She didn't even notice. I cry a lot these days.

Won't somebody help me, please?

Yes, there is help.

This material helped Joan and it can help you, too. I know this because of my experience as a caregiver and as a professional in the field of aging.

I graduated from Northwestern University in Evanston, Illinois with a degree in counseling psychology and a concentration in gerontology, the study of aging. While working in Philadelphia at the Center for the

Study of Adult Development, I pioneered a seminar geared to helping the families of the aged. The seminar was funded by the Dolfinger-McMahon Foundation and the Pew Charitable Trust. A pilot program of seminars for family caregivers was conducted.

After several successful seminars, former participants and I founded the National Support Center for Families of the Aging. We then co-authored both a workbook and leader's manual to enable others to carry out the mission.

I left the Support Center to work as the National Director of Ministry for the Aging for the American Baptists in Valley Forge, Pennsylvania. In that position I encouraged congregations to offer the seminar and provided many workshops to teach others to lead their own seminars.

During that time, however, my own parents were aging. In fact, I took a six-week leave to return to Minnesota and help my mother care for my father at home in his last weeks. Since then I have helped my mother, who was sixty-seven at that time, through surgeries and moves until the present. She is now 100 and has been living in a care center since she was ninety-seven.

What that means is that I have both professional and personal knowledge about what it means to be a caregiver. I understand the feelings and frustrations involved in caregiving. I, too, have banged my head against the unforgiving wall of aging losses for my parent while dealing with my own aging process.

Statistics show that the family caregiver is typically forty-six years old, the exact age I was when I cared for my father. What the statistics don't show is that now, at age seventy-seven, I am *still* caring for an aging parent! Wow! How's that for a powerful number? I have been involved in this process for *thirty years* and am still going! Fortunately I have a brother and a sister who are fully involved and they cover for me when I'm not able to be there for my mother.

If our Joan has this long period of caregiving to look forward to, how will she handle it? Maybe we shouldn't tell her. You think?

So, how *do* we handle this long period of caregiving? In the following chapters I will share insights and methods that have helped others and will, hopefully, help you as well.

To begin, I am going to ask you to start a journal. Now, no groaning about writing. Journaling has been shown to be a major stress reliever. Something about getting your feelings out on paper seems to be even better, sometimes, than telling a friend.

I think this benefit comes from the fact that in a journal you can be totally honest. No one will ever see the things you write (unless you want them to), things that might cause you guilt or shame. Writing in a journal is like telling *yourself* how you feel and what your hopes and dreams are. Pouring one's heart out in a journal can leave you feeling emptied, almost purified. Sometimes new insights emerge as you write. It's as if seeing your thoughts and feelings *in writing* gives you a second chance to experience them before they are whisked away on the wings of time.

As an excellent stress reliever, journaling can also help alleviate stress symptoms such as high blood pressure, high blood sugar and other major causes of ill health. Keeping this journal will help you express your feelings, work through your problems and thus lower your stress levels.

If you question these claims, go online and do your own research. There are sites that are geared specifically toward caregivers and their issues.

Journaling will also help you track your progress through this book. At the end of each chapter, there will be one or more exercises for you to do.

Here's the first one:

Exercise 1

Go to a stationery store and buy an easy-writing pen and a notebook. Make sure the notebook is big enough for you to write comfortably on the surface when you don't have a table. I always get tablets that have an extra strong cardboard backing and a binding that allows me to fold the cover back. Then I can write on my lap in airplanes or on park benches or while waiting in doctors' offices (where caregivers spend a lot of time, by the way).

Just start writing about anything at all. Write anything that comes to mind even if it's pretty nasty. *It is for your eyes alone.* Only by keeping it private can you make sure you will be totally honest on the page. If you feel the need to lock the journal up so no one in your family sees it, then do so. You can also go back and tear out pages and burn them or shred them. But first write the most honest responses you can.

Here's a question to get you started:

What would you like to change in your life today?

Just keep writing for three pages. When finished, go on to Chapter 2, in which we will discover the nature of Joan's *real* problem and perhaps yours as well.

Figure 1*

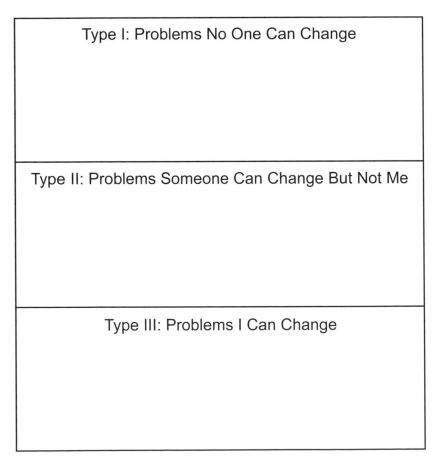

What Is the Real Problem?

How to Discover the Real Problem

So, what is Joan's basic problem? This is important, because if we can't define the problem there is no hope of solving it.

By looking at Figure 1, on the facing page, you will see that it is helpful to organize problems into three types:

- Type I is a problem that no one can change;
- Type II is a problem that someone may be able to change — but not you; and
- Type III is a problem that you can actually do something about.

Where is Joan in this chart?

Type I Problems

In Figure 1-A, on the next page, we see that Joan has a *Type I* problem, at least in part. *Joan's mother is getting old.* This may be sad, but it is something about which Joan can do nothing. It is simply a fact of life.

Figure 1-A: Joan

Type I: Problems No One Can Change *Joan's mother is getting old and can no longer live by herself.*
Type II: Problems Someone Can Change But Not Joan *Joan's husband and children could take more of the responsibility for Joan's mother.*
Type III: Problems Joan Can Change *Joan brings her mother to live with her.*

If no one can do anything about it, why is it such a problem?

It's because *Type I* problems have *feelings* attached to them.

Have you ever seen a picture of those big sharks swimming around in the sea with all those little fish attached to them? Those little fish are called parasites. We have lots of *parasite* feelings attached to our *Type I* problems. These little parasites wreak havoc on our ability to solve our big problems.

In a later chapter we'll address these issues and see how Joan can better deal with them.

For now, let's address Marilyn's problems.

Type II Problems

When Marilyn walked into one of my seminars, she boiled over with resentment. During our first guided meditation, she blurted out, "I hate her! I hate her. I hate her!"

In the debriefing sessions she admitted to having these negative feelings toward one of her three sisters. Marilyn had taken her mother into her home when her mother could no longer care for herself. Now Marilyn needed help, and her closest sister, Helga, had said, "You made your bed. Now you can lie in it. You took Mom into your home when we thought another solution would be better. Now you're stuck with your decision."

So, Marilyn was stuck with these problems:

Type I: an invalid mother, *a problem no one can change*, and

Type II: uncooperative sisters, *a problem that her sisters could change, but not Marilyn.*

Some people resort to laying guilt on their siblings until they capitulate, a strategy that usually results in the death of the relationship. I recall one person who put his parent on a plane then called his sibling to tell her to pick her parent up at the airport. That sort of drastic action is definitely not recommended.

The intense emotion and frustration involved in trying to get someone else to do what you think is right is debilitating, demoralizing and downright ugly. Trying to control the behavior of others is almost always a lose/lose situation.

In Marilyn's case she not only lost her relationship with a sister, who was formerly her favorite, but also lost her view of herself as a loving, caring person. Hating her sister was not an acceptable outcome — a lose/lose if ever there was one.

Type III Problems

But through insights Marilyn discovered in the seminar, she had an idea. Wonder of wonders. She was not helpless after all. She had a choice. Maybe several choices.

Type III: a problem Marilyn could change. *She could hire someone to help out, since her sisters wouldn't or couldn't.*

The next time her sister called, a strange woman answered the phone.

"Where is Marilyn?" her sister demanded.

"Who wants to know?" the woman answered.

"Her sister, Helga."

"I think she's out shopping. I'm not sure."

"Well, who are you?" Helga once again demanded.

"I'm the home care nurse she hired so she can have three afternoons a week off."

"That must be expensive. Marilyn doesn't have a lot of extra money."

"Oh, she's not paying me. Your mother is."

Helga's indignation came right through the phone line. "So, what are you doing for my mother right now?"

"Right now? I'm playing pinochle with her, and she's beating me. Gotta go. Bye now." The line went dead.

Sweet (as my son would say). Kind of a satisfying way to remake that bed of Marilyn's and also relieve her stress.

So, there it was: a Type III problem — a situation *in which Marilyn can take some action herself.* She did what she had to do. She defined the part of the big problem that she could take responsibility for and then acted. She may still deal with guilt, anger, resentment and frustration, but she will know she is doing everything she can realistically be expected to do.

Figure 1-B: Joan and Marilyn

Type I: Problems No One Can Change

*Joan's mother is getting old and
can no longer live by herself.*

Marilyn's mother can no longer live alone.

Type II: Problems Someone Can Change But Not Them

Joan's family could do more.

*Marilyn's sisters don't agree with her solution
so they won't help take care of their mother.*

Type III: Problems They Can Change

Joan brings her mother to live with her.

*Marilyn hires a home care nurse
three afternoons a week.*

Review

Let's review the three types of problems: the first, as in Joan's situation in Chapter I, is a problem that no one can fix; the second is one that someone can fix but not necessarily *you;* and, the third is a problem or part of a problem that you can do something about. Figure 1-B shows Joan's and Marilyn's problems on the chart.

So what kind of problem are you trying to fix? Are you banging your head against the brick wall of aging, trying to turn back the clock? Are you losing sleep while you try to figure out how to manipulate your siblings into helping you do an impossible task? Or are you defining one part of the problem, a piece you can actually do something about, and doing something about it?

Exercise 2

Journaling

Before we move on, take out your journal and make a chart that looks like Figure 1.

Now look at *your* situation and fill the chart in with your own problems, as we did for Marilyn. Are you concentrating on the *Type III* problem or wasting time on *Type I*?

Spend some time with this before you move on.

Express Yourself

As we said when we talked about Joan and Marilyn, each one of those situations involves feelings. Feelings you can do something about.

"Oh, yeah," you say, "and what is that?"

Well, feelings are meant to be *felt*. You have a right to your feelings. You can try denying them, but it won't work. Stuff them down and they'll turn up in your big toe. Hide them, and they'll pop out in anger at the people you love the most — or at a party when you throw a wine glass at a plate glass window — or some other embarrassing *faux pas*. So just *feel* them.

Remember when Joan said she "cried later for about two hours"? Good for Joan. You can cry, too. Or like Marilyn you can scream out your feelings in an appropriate place (probably not a prayer meeting). One seminar participant admitted that, after every visit with her mother in the nursing home, she rolled up the car windows and screamed all the way home. I recommend that procedure as technically brilliant. You can feel whatever it is you are feeling, whether it is positive or negative. *You have a right to your feelings.* (But remember, while it's okay to have negative feelings; it's not always okay to act on them. Just because you want to smash your sister's favorite china plates, it's probably not a good idea, especially if they're family heirlooms.)

Beware Shoulds and Ought tos

Most important of all, don't let other folks tell you what you *should* feel. Any statement that begins with "You should . . . " or "You ought to . . . " needs to be tuned out immediately. However, I don't recommend hitting the speaker over the head with the bed pan, although — on second thought — *no, not really.*

Seek Fellow Sufferers

It's easier to express your feelings if you have people to help you, and I highly recommend support groups in that instance (but it is not essential). Use your journal, use this book, send me an email, or best of all, find at least one other person who is going through what you are going through.

Share your feelings with people who are struggling and who are honest enough to admit it. Remember: Struggling folks can learn and grow. Surround yourself with them. If necessary and you can afford it, see a therapist who knows this area of stress. Read books and, if it's your habit, pray for insight as to where the feelings come from. And always remember, *you are doing the best you can do.* Take a deep breath and say this over to yourself:

"I am doing the best I can do."

Yes, you absolutely are. You are doing the very best you know how to do. Honor that. Honor yourself.

Feel the feelings, acknowledge them, honor them, and release them. Don't wallow around in them. Remember, your feelings do not control you. You are in charge.

Figure 2*: YOU

Type I Problems No One Can Change:	Feelings About This:
Type II Problems that Can Be Changed by Someone But Not by Me:	Feelings About This:
Type III Problems with Elements I Can Change:	Feelings About This:

* Do not write in this book if you borrowed it from a library. The publisher grants permission for you to photocopy this page for your personal use.

Avoid the Deluded

On the other hand, if you meet someone who says, "Oh, I just love having Mom live with us. Such a blessing to have her still here." Or if someone tells you: "Dad asked to go to the retirement home; he really doesn't like cooking and cleaning, and he's so happy there," run like the hounds of hell are on your heels. These folks will not give you the support you need.

Don't share your feelings with someone who lives in la-la land, or whose family is perfect, or who is so delusional that they may explode at any minute, showering you with their shrapnel.

Chart Your Problems

So now we can finish the chart in Figure 2: YOU. Use the information for Marilyn in Figure 1-B as your guidelines.

Put in your feelings. And note an important fact: *you are not helpless.* Of the six rectangles in the six-square grid in Figure 2, you can do something about four of them. That's two thirds in anybody's book. So, congratulations. You are in control.

If your response to the above is a resounding "Sez you!" then maybe this next section will help you. We will start the charts upside down. (No, no, turn the book right side up. I didn't mean it literally.)

What if we come at the problem asking this question: *What am I doing in this situation that nobody else can do?* (Type III)

Second question: *What am I doing in this situation that someone else could do?* (Type II)

Third question: *What am I doing that no one needs to do or can do?* (Type I)

Here's a good example of a *Type III* problem that meets the criteria. (If you're not a Christian you can skip this paragraph or read it as a comment on a legend.) I remember studying the crucifixion and wondering why Jesus had to die on the cross. It seemed somewhat extreme to say the least. The answer was simple: He was the only one who had the power to save us. *Only he* could perform the sacrifice that was needed. From that lesson came my mantra:

Am I the only one who can do this?

What I Did

When my own father was dying, I had the opportunity to put into practice much of what I was teaching others. My mother wanted to bring Dad home from the hospital so he could die in the house he had built for his family with his own hands. At the time I was the only sibling with the freedom to help. Although I lived in Pennsylvania and my parents lived in northern Minnesota, I had others who could take over my responsibilities with our non-profit National Support Center for Families of the Aging.

My sister in Wisconsin had two children, one in school, one in pre-school. My brother lived in Alaska and had two teenaged girls. My youngest child was in boarding school in Maine. I had the freedom and financial resources to respond. I helped my mother for the last three weeks of Dad's life and stayed with her for three weeks after his death. At that time, *I was the only one who could do it.* Being there with them during this special time blessed me in powerful ways.

Finish Your Exercise

So, now do your homework. Fill in the charts. Admit to some of those negative feelings and put them into your chart. Answer the three questions on the previous page and make sure you are not "pouring your energy down a rat hole," as my former colleague, Jane Dewey Heald, used to say about useless and wasted effort.

Actions that Heal

Begin making lists of ways you can deal with your feelings. Talking things out with a friend is often therapeutic, but select the friend carefully. Try some new things: watch old movies with your parent, especially funny ones (my sister and her daughter watch Victor Borge videos when things get rough) or watch without your parent — watching tear-jerkers gives you an excellent opportunity to cry, getting some of that sorrow out of your system.

Go online to search out resources for others taking care of parents. Appendix D: States' Websites on Aging is a good place to start (there's a listing for Canada too). Every one of the fifty states has an agency on aging, and many offer links to county and city resources.

Go to a bookstore or your local library to find other books on care-giving. Talk to your librarian about borrowing books for you from other libraries. Suggest that your church start a support group. Put a little of that American ingenuity to work.

And now I'll see you next in the Responsibility Circle. Unlike the Dress Circle at the opera, no tie or tux required.

Chapter 3

Who's Been Eating
My Responsibility Pie?

One evening as I worked in my home office I received a frantic call from a man named John. His indignant voice said that his mother's doctor had notified him that an *intervention* was needed on behalf of his mother. Our call went something like this:

"So what's the problem, John?"

"What's the problem? What's the problem?" Sputtering and harrumphing on the line. "The problem is she was a h . . . of a mother. She remarried, and that son-of-a b . . . . used the strap on me every chance he got. She just stood by. If I defied her, she sicced him on me. Sometimes they both beat on me at the same time. What's the problem? I'll tell you what's the problem? I hate that old b . . . . !"

"So, what's the problem, John?"

Pause.

Silence reigned at the end of the line. Some more sputtering, a sob. "Isn't it obvious?" he asked, his voice harsh and raspy.

"It is to me, but not, I think, to you, John. The next time the doctor or the social worker calls, you could say, 'John Smith?

Never heard of him' or 'John Smith is on a mule trip to Outer Mongolia' or 'John Smith died.' " (I prefer the Outer Mongolia trip to being dead. But then, that's just me.)

"I can't do that . . . I wish I could, but I can't." The anguish in his voice could've broken a heart or two.

"And *that's* the problem, John. Even though she abandoned you, you can't abandon her. It's tough. It's not fair. But that's the way it is."

"So what can I do?"

"I can't tell you what to do, but I can give you some information to help you. Okay? Are you listening?"

"Hanging on your every word!"

Honest Emotions

When a caregiver is honest about feelings, they can learn and grow. That's what I love about working with caregivers. They are desperate enough to listen, learn and grow. My energy isn't going to waste; it's being put to use by folks who appreciate it.

So, what *does* John need to consider?

First of all, whether he likes it or not, John doesn't want to run into his mother pushing a grocery cart full of all her belongings down the middle of the street the next time he goes out to shop. Nor does he want to get a call from the police saying they found her curled up over a heating vent on the sidewalk. He feels some *responsibility* for her, even if he doesn't love her.

Old Issues

That is not as uncommon as you might think. John's case is extreme, but many caregivers have issues with their care receiver. Some hope to resolve issues by giving care: "She always loved my brother best, but now she'll have to love me best," and on and on.

The reasons are almost infinite.

Figure 3

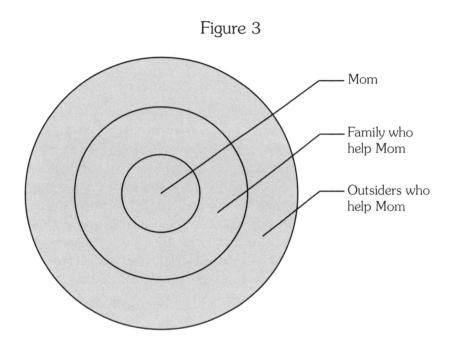

- Mom
- Family who help Mom
- Outsiders who help Mom

Who's Responsible?

Another way we can help John is to look at his mother as the center of a circle. Around her are all the people who have some responsibility for her care. I like to think in terms of financial, emotional and physical care. Who do you think should inhabit John's mother's circle?

Now is the time to look at Figure 3.

Using the following list and any others you can think of, fill in the circle: doctor, lawyer, banker, social worker, siblings, grandchildren, friends, other relatives, church friends or club friends.

But here's the clincher: How many of you put John's mother in the responsibility circle? I don't mean in the center, but somewhere, as one of the folks who have responsibility for her financial, emotional and physical well being? After all, in the long run, we are responsible for *our own* well being. If we fall down on the job or can't do it for reasons of illness or age, then others need to step in.

Planning

Ultimately, no one is responsible for someone else's lack of planning and foresight. Our society tells us otherwise, but it's important for our own future to keep that in mind. Believe me, caring for your aging relative should be the best motivation for planning for your own future. *If you don't plan it, someone else will, and you might not like their plan.*

Obviously, John's mother has not planned. She is alone and unloved. So what is John's role in her care? Since he didn't go to Outer Mongolia when he had the chance, he must have some feelings about this issue. So, let's look at what is necessary for John to do to live with himself. Because that's what we are talking about here.

John has to be true to himself and his values, whatever his feelings are about his mother.

Needs *versus* Wants

Let's assume John has done everything that is necessary. He has found an assisted living unit where his mother gets her meals and has the company of other women. She is aided during bath times and her medications are supervised. She takes the local transport bus to shop or go out for a meal.

Yet when John visits his mother, she is unhappy. She complains about the food, doesn't like the other women, doesn't like going outside to smoke (in a heated gazebo, yet) and wants more booze (limited to two drinks per day).

That is where John has to differentiate between *needs* and *wants*. You know how that goes. You buy a new car. You *want* a Lexus, but you get what you *need* — a Ford. You *need* a break. You *want* a cruise of the Greek Islands but you settle for what you can afford — a ride on the Staten Island Ferry. Your *need* is met, not your *want*.

Yes, John's mother *wants* it all. And she *wants* someone else to organize and pay for it. She *wants* John to forget his horrific upbringing and "act like a more loving son." Well, he can't. In this case he can meet her *needs* — her actual needs for shelter, food, social activity — but her horrific mothering blew her chance to have her *wants* met as well.

John's mother, like many aged and ill care receivers, is a bottomless pit of need and want. There may be no end to what they will demand, if given the opportunity. And that's okay for them. They can't be expected to sort out what John should do; that's just too much to expect of the vulnerable. So who decides? John, of course. He is the one who must determine his involvement and the amount of his life that he is willing to expend on this. And he can do this by *setting limits*.

Setting Limits, Meeting Needs

Setting limits is the key to success in caregiving. Needy care receivers can suck up all your outer and inner resources, leaving you with nothing for your present or your own aging future. Giving people options is one way of limiting the demands on your time and energy.

Let's say that Mom calls and says, "Sweetie, I need to go to the store today. When can you pick me up?"

Since you took her to the store yesterday and had other commitments for today, it is definitely not in your plan. A good answer might be, "Gee, Mom, I already have plans for today. How about if I pick you up on Wednesday, and we go shopping then?"

"I think I need some stuff today," Mom growls.

"Tell me what you need, and I can pick it up for you later today."

Silence.

"So what do you need?"

Mom's needs are being met and so are yours. It's not a total win/win, but it's not a lose/lose either. Sometimes that is the best we can hope for.

Often one need cloaks a want. Maybe Mom doesn't actually *need* anything at the store, but she is lonely and *wants* some attention. In a later chapter we will discuss listening for these cloaked needs and how they can be met.

Exercise 3

So get out your journal and make a list of your relative's *needs* on one side and *wants* on the other. If you can fulfill both needs and wants, great. If you can't, don't beat yourself up. Remember, *you are doing the best you can do.*

Your Life's Pie

Now, draw a circle that represents your own life. Imagine that this circle is a pie and draw lines radiating out from the center, until you have different-sized pie slices showing all the people you have some responsibility for: spouse, children, grandchildren, your siblings, your job, your house, your community service (or church), your neighbors and, of course, your parent(s).

How big a piece of the pie is your parent taking right now? Because of unusual circumstances, this slice might be bigger than it normally would be. But here is the important point: *No one is entitled to eat your whole pie! No one!*

So if you find that your relative is taking up your whole life, especially if it has been going on for a long time, then something is wrong. I repeat: *No one is entitled to eat your whole pie!*

You might want to draw a responsibility circle for yourself, too. Put yourself in the center and see who comes to mind as being able to take some responsibility for your financial, emotional and physical well being.

Don't forget that you are ultimately responsible for yourself. That is especially important for you just now. Don't expect to be rescued; no one is going to come galloping in on a white horse and carry you off to those Greek Islands. If you want it badly enough, you'll have to get there on your own.

Your Needs Come First

This is where you become a tight-rope walker. You have to do a balancing act between your needs and the needs of your relative and everyone else in your life. Remember how the airline always tells you to put your own oxygen mask on first and then your child's mask? If you passed out, who would put on your child's mask?

The same principle applies here. If you ruin your health, destroy your relationships with siblings and/or spouse, and you end up needing care yourself, then where will your relative be? *Take care of your own needs. No one else will do it.* Well, that's not quite true. Others may help if you *need* it but maybe not the way you *want* it.

Now you have all this wisdom. Piece of cake from now on, right? Oops, wrong. You're still stuck? Let's look at what may be holding you back:

Could you be stuck in the big bog?

Chapter 4

Help! I'm Stuck in the Big Bog!

Two months after the seminar ended, one of our participants, Phyllis, walked in the front door of her home with steam coming out of her ears. Without saying hello to her husband, she began her rant:

"I can't believe that place. Do you know what I found to-day? I found Mother sitting in her wheel chair in an old house coat, her hair in tangles and her nylons rolled down to her ankles above her house slippers. Mother never appeared in public like that. I'm livid. I shouted and raved until they sent an aid to help me dress her properly."

As Phyllis stopped for breath, her husband looked her straight in the eye and said, "You flunked that seminar!"

"What? What did you say?"

"I said, 'You flunked that seminar.' "

But he was wrong.

Phyllis had attended every session. She participated in every exercise. She shared and listened when appropriate. What had she missed? Nothing. She hadn't missed a thing. So what was going on? Phyllis was caught and held fast in what I call the *Big Bog of parentcare*.

The actual Big Bog is a Minnesota State Recreation Area that includes a 500-square-mile peat bog, the largest in the lower 48 states. Recently I read a description written by Barbara Greiner, a writer who had to walk through the bog: "We sank in the moss as deep as our legs were long. Every step required immense effort in order to wrench each foot and leg free from the clinging moss, swing it high over the near waist level moss and take another step."*

Is that how you feel sometimes? Like you are pulling yourself up and out of clinging muck with every step? If so, you are caught in the *Big Bog*, sinking in the *emotional quicksand* called *parentcare*.

Focus on Solutions

What if I were to tell you that the chances are nine out of ten that I could solve your parentcare dilemma in about fifteen minutes? Would you believe me? No? Well, maybe I am exaggerating a little. But in general, almost anyone who has knowledge of local resources, medical establishments and current laws could solve your problem with very little effort. That includes people like social workers, doctors, nurses, priests and pastors — and even annoying friends (people like Mr. and Mrs. U. Should).

Yes, But

Let's imagine for a minute or two that Dave is in my office, telling me his problem. Dave says, "I can't stand living with my Dad any longer."

My answer, "Well, that's easy to fix. I know an assisted living community he would love."

Dave's answer (and if it doesn't start with "Yes, but," then he isn't the person I think he is): "Yes, but Dad doesn't like apartment living . . . or city living . . . or won't be moved . . . or hates people . . ." And Dave and I are back where we started; the *yes, buts* have defeated us for the umpteenth time.

They defeat us because they have on their side all the *swamp things* in the Big Bog, which is, in many cases, the result of a lifetime of obedience,

---

* from "The swamp was so dark they called it 'bog tea.'" *Northern Student*, the newspaper of Bemidji State University in Minnesota.

independence and love (or hate or something in between). After all, our relationship with our parents is *the oldest relationship we have.*

It's About You

Having said all that, I'm going to ask you to do some difficult tasks. Hopefully, throughout this book, you have made some progress in identifying your feelings and your actual problems and responsibilities.

I hope you have noticed that this book is not about your parent. It's about you, and it will always be about you. Your parent is almost peripheral in this situation. Parentcare is the ultimate exercise in personal responsibility. This is one area where only you can do what you have to do to rescue yourself.

Rescue Yourself

So how do we get out of the Big Bog? *We understand that we have choices!* Many people come to my seminars saying, "I have no choice." Oh, yes, you do. You may reject the choices you have, but they are there. Even *not doing something* is a choice. *Rejecting an option* is a choice. You can even choose to stay stuck in the Big Bog if you like frogs and snakes and mosquitoes. (I prefer the mule trip to Outer Mongolia if I'm going to be stuck somewhere, but, again, that's just me.)

In our seminar this is the point at which, one by one, the participants take center stage, state their situation (which most of us know anyway after eight weeks of interaction in small groups) and *asks* us to brainstorm solutions for them. One member takes notes, which are later given to the center-stage participant. (This works well in a support group.)

The key is *no comments or questions or yes buts are allowed. There is only listening, and, hopefully that with an open mind.*

Participants then take the notes home and investigate each option as best they can, whether or not they actually think they might use it.

Now here's another funny thing about human nature. Let's say you go to the library, look up local resources, find the ideal day care situation for your mom — a place for her to be safe and happy while you're at work. You take her there, and she loves it. It's an absolutely perfect solution.

You rush to tell your pastor about it. You are puzzled when she looks at you with a mystified expression.

"What's wrong?" you ask.

"That's exactly the place I suggested to you three weeks ago," she replies. "You rejected it."

Aren't we strange creatures?

Exercise 4

Because we are strange, unpredictable creatures who are occasionally blinded and frightened by our fears and prejudices, your assignment for this chapter is to go out into your community and investigate your resources. (Groaning and moaning is allowed — as long as you do the exercise anyway.) Everything from parks and libraries to adult day care, from supervised living to home health care, from counseling services to hospice services. Remember, *you are only an investigator.* (It helps to pretend that you are doing this for someone else, a friend or relative. Sometimes you need that distance to gain any objectivity on the issue.)

I suggest that, if your parent is living in your home, you *not* have things mailed to the house unless they come, like pornography, in a plain brown envelope with no return address. Better your mom should suspect that you are titillating yourself with *Playgirl* than thinking about moving her out.

After all this, you may decide that the best solution is the one you already have. And that's okay. Don't "fuss yourself," as they say in the South. I'm quite sure you will never feel quite the same pressures again.

The parentcare process is never easy; however, it can be rewarding. Working through the issues brought up while caring for an aging parent can initiate a tremendous time of growth in your life. Don't lose this chance to deepen insight into your own actions and to understand others with more clarity and, perhaps, more empathy. And remember to use it as an opportunity to plan for your old age.

The next chapter will help you identify those forces that are aligned against you — the forces that hold you in place — that can actually imprison you.

Chapter 5

What Is Holding Me Back?

Vera came to the seminar knowing there was a solution for her mother's situation.

"I know," she told us in the first meeting, "that if my mother sold her house, she would have enough money to move to that assisted living apartment I took her to see. *But* my mother didn't like it. She wants to stay in her own home."

Vera would love to have her mother living *independently* in the community.

"The problem is that staying in her own home requires the services of Meals on Wheels, and she doesn't like the food so I end up cooking for her; a weekly nurse's visit for bathing; three visits a day from me so that I can supervise her meds; and countless trips — in my car — to the doctor, dentist and laboratory for blood draws. My own life has disappeared."

The Immovable Wall

Maybe you're feeling like that now. You have read the first four chapters. You have found some relief in knowing you are not alone. You have found clues to what's going on. You recognize that you are stuck in the Big Bog. You may even have discovered that you are trying to make someone happy who was never happy in the first place. But you still feel like you are pushing against an immovable wall. No matter how much you push, the wall doesn't move.

So let's look at what we'll call the *pushing forces* and the *holding forces*.

The Pushing Forces

The pushing forces are all the positives that exist in this situation. These are things like your desire to be a good daughter, your husband's cooperation, the help of your children and the support of community services you are using.

The big problem is: No matter how many *pushing forces* exist, unless you can remove some of the *holding forces*, the wall cannot move.

Think of a bobber, a moveable plug. Unless the pressure is released from above, the bobber won't move up no matter how much pressure is exerted from below. Stronger pushing only increases the pressure, making you more and more stressed.

The Holding Forces

So, the first order of business is to identify the forces holding the wall in place — no mean feat in itself. But some are relatively obvious: lack of suitable facilities for Vera's mother, lack of time to look for suitable facilities, Vera's guilt about making her mother unhappy, Mom's resistance, and Vera's need to please her pastor — these are just a few possibilities.

Instead of looking at it from the point of view of Vera's mother and her situation, let's look at what *Vera* gets out of it. What is she trying to accomplish by letting her mother control her life?

One day during Vera's meditations in the seminar she realized that she *was trying to get the approval from her mother that she never had growing up* — and she also realized that she never would get it, not this way or any other way.

Wow!

Vera's need for her mother's approval has given her mother control over Vera's life. Maybe Vera will continue behaving in the same way as before, but let me tell you it will never *feel* the same again. Vera will grieve the loss of hope for Mom's approval. She may grieve for the loss of those sporadic pats on the head. But that particular *holding force* has been vanquished, beaten, drubbed, taken out. No more automatic responses to cries for help. Now Vera's brain can take over, not her hidden emotions. She still wants the best for her mother. That hasn't changed. But now Vera wants the best for *both* of them.

It is not always possible. Sometimes the best for Mom may not be best for Vera and vice versa. But Vera, like you, is resilient, resourceful, inventive and smart. Now that the particular holding force — the *need for Mom's approval and love* — has been pulled away and is no longer holding her back, Vera can figure out what she *needs* to do.

Control

Marta came to the seminar with a different situation. She moved her mother from her little cottage on the lake into the local retirement apartments. Now Marta could relax because her mother was safe during the snowy winters. As spring neared, her mother became more and more depressed.

During the following exercise, Marta's response to one of the statements showed her that she was trying to solve the problem by controlling her mother. In fact, she was behaving just like her mother had behaved. By moving her mother from her cottage, in spite of her protests, Marta was trying to control her mother's life just like her mother had tried to control Marta's life.

This was a powerful holding force for Marta. In giving up the *need* to control her mother, she freed herself to seek a mutually satisfying solution: Her mother spent winter in the apartment and moved to the cottage for the summer.

Hurray! Marta — 1; holding forces — 0.

So far in this chapter, you've heard others' stories. Now is the time for *you* to get to work.

Exercise 5

Below is a list of open ended statements. I want you to finish these statements, but only when you can be completely relaxed, alone and undisturbed for at least thirty minutes.

Relax

If you meditate, that would be a good way to begin this exercise. Some people relax with prayer. Some people close their eyes and see themselves descending a long stairway. Some people count down from ten.

You do whatever it takes to relax *you*.

If you don't have a standard way to relax, follow these simple guidelines:

Find a comfortable place to sit where you can be alone and quiet. Close your eyes.

Breathe in and out, deeply, several times. On each outgoing breath, tell yourself that all tension and stress is going out with the breath.

Starting with the top of your head, feel the tension drain away down your body and out through your toes. Move to your neck and shoulders, feel that tension drain away through your toes. Do this for your whole body, paying special attention to your abdomen as tension tends to pool there and keep you knotted up.

When you feel like a wet noodle, pick up this book and finish the statements on the facing page. If you feel the tension again, stop until the wet noodle is back and continue. When a particular statement ending strikes you as important, you may need to stop and write it down to be positive you remember it when you finish the exercise.

Write your responses in your journal. Don't edit. You don't need to punctuate or spell correctly, just relax and write. If nothing comes into your mind after a few seconds, just move on to the next statement.

When you have gone through all the statements, slowly come back to the present by wiggling your toes and fingers, then moving your feet, legs and arms. If necessary, count backward from ten. At the count of one you will be fully restored to your typical uncooked noodle state.

Complete These Statements:

My aging parent wants . . .

It's just not practical for my parent to . . .

I haven't been able to find . . .

One resource I sure wish I had is . . .

These days I never seem to have enough . . .

I've been taught I should always . . .

The quotation my head keeps repeating is . . .

I feel guilty that I don't really want . . .

By myself I can't . . .

It makes me furious when . . .

If I defy my parent . . .

It's ungrateful to . . .

I really need . . .

What I really want is . . .

I wish I had never promised . . .

Everybody in the family acts like they expect . . .

Ever since I was small, I always . . .

I would feel ashamed if . . .

In my heart, I am comparing myself to . . .

What does my parent really want from me . . .

What do I want from my parent . . .

I'm longing for . . .

I pray for the courage to try . . .

My religious tradition teaches me that . . .

My parent always wanted to control my life, and I always . . .

Part of me is not willing to share the care of my parent with . . .

If I didn't have this problem with my parent, I would . . .

I would feel neglectful if I didn't . . .

One mistake I never want to make is . . .

The person whose good opinion I most cherish is . . .

When you have finished and have come back to the present time, put your responses aside for at least an hour. Do something totally different. Later, come back to your journal and see what you have written. It may surprise you.

By the way, what statement do you think opened Marta's eyes to her holding force? Vera's?

This was a tough chapter. You may have gone deeper than you expected. You may even be startled by some of your responses. You may want to repeat the exercise. You might want to let your insights sit for a while.

When you're ready, move on to the next chapter, in which you will learn a skill that will serve you well for the rest of your life.

Chapter 6

Are You Listening to the Real Message?

Meet Maxine and her sister, Iris. Their mother has died and Maxine is caring for her father. She is the only one who lives nearby and is also a widow herself. Let's take a peek at some of their correspondence.

Dear Iris,

I'm enclosing a list of the jewelry and a few other small items that Mother left. Dad says we should divide them up between us. I have starred the ones I want, mostly because I gave them to her at some point or because she told me it would be mine. However, since you're the next oldest daughter, I think you should have the next choice and then pass it on to the boys' wives. If you have any problem about any of it, please let me know.

Dad is at home now and seems to be managing. I go over every day and fix him a good lunch, and he comes over for dinner about three times a week and spends most of his weekends with us. The kids send their love and so do I.

Love, Maxine

Dear Iris,

I'm sure I can't figure out why you're so angry about the list I sent. I did not take anything without telling you or without asking Dad. Mom had given me the brooch and the pearl necklace the month before she died. She said she wanted me to have them because I had spent so much time helping her and taking care of her. I haven't asked Dad about anything because he gets so upset. And if he thought we were fighting about it, his heart would break. I don't know what Janet thinks I've taken, and I can't see that it's any of her business. After all, she's only an in-law. If any of you want to come down here and help clean up this house and deal with Dad and all his stuff, you're welcome.

Maxine

(Months later)

Dear Iris,

It was such fun having you here even for a short time. You were a tremendous help the day of the big house sale, and it was even fun having a good cry with you after that family took away our old piano. I still remember the hours we played chopsticks on that old thing. I thank God that you were here to help.

Love, Maxine

Let's go back to Maxine and Iris and eavesdrop on a conversation they had shortly after Iris arrived to help with the house sale. They had begun to talk about their mother, and the subject of their misunderstanding about pieces of her jewelry came up. See if you can tell if one of them has taken a course in listening. If so, which one?

Maxine: "Remember the letter I wrote to you about the jewelry?"
Iris: "I sure do, I was really upset."
Maxine: "I guess you were."
Iris: "Yes, when I read that letter I could just see red. I was so mad."

Maxine: "Oh, boy. I really made you mad."

Iris: "Yes, because it seemed you were just taking over everything here."

Maxine: "You felt I was just taking over?"

Iris: "I guess I was angry because I really wanted to be here with you — and I couldn't."

Maxine: "You wanted to help."

Iris: "I sure did. But I knew that I couldn't so I was angry and I guess I took it out on you. I'm really sorry about that."

Maxine: "That's okay. I understand now that you were really feeling bad that you couldn't be here to help and that you weren't really angry with me."

Iris: "I wasn't really mad at you. In fact, I guess I was a little jealous because you could be here to help Dad and I couldn't. I remember when we were kids sometimes I used to think you were his favorite. Maybe that's what really made me angry."

Maxine: "That's really funny because I used to think you were his favorite!"

Iris: "I guess the truth is that he didn't have favorites. He loved us all the same." (Pause) "I sure do miss him — the way he was before, I mean." (Pause) "Do you remember?"

Active Listening

Message coded, decoded and delivered. Seems easy, doesn't it? It's not easy, though. Do you know why? Because Iris didn't know what the message was either. She needed help to find out where that anger was coming from. All she knew was that she was angry. Only with a *real* listener could she decode her own message.

There is another requirement: The process takes two people who want to listen and be listened to.

Sometimes we don't really want to find out what's wrong. We just want to express our anger, have a good fight and then go on about our business, leaving the other person with the anger and frustration we felt. That's called *dumping,* and that's not what we're learning here.

It's easy for us to confuse real listening with just being physically present when someone else is speaking. Usually the only person we're fooling is ourselves; our body language, our verbal responses, our general attitude, all show the speaker that we are not really hearing what's being said.

Listening is a skill, and there are ways to let others know we are really listening to them. In the next pages, you'll get some pointers on how to listen. Pay attention because you get to practice next.

Body Language

Since our bodies speak, use yours to speak for you. Sit facing your aged parent, maintain comfortable eye contact and lean forward in an attentive attitude. (Note: In some cultures eye contact is disrespectful. Do what is comfortable and appropriate for you.) Resist the distractions of children or roommates or husbands or wives or televisions, and for some span of time — maybe only five minutes — focus on the person.

It is especially easy in nursing homes to be distracted by the nurses' conversations, your elder's roommate, the ever present TV. Usually the nursing home atmosphere makes us uncomfortable, uneasy, sad or scared. It is so much more comfortable to let our minds wander away from the parent who has to live there. It is painful to hear the complaints or the pleading, "I want to go home. Why can't I go home?" So we let our minds wander. By focusing on the person and resisting distractions, we are saying "I love you" with our bodies.

Touching

The sense of touch plays an important role for us throughout our entire lives. As infants, children and later as someone in an intimate sexual relationship, the sense of touch gives us important cues as to how others are feeling about us, and we in turn give messages to them. The aged have an even greater need for this sense, as many of their other senses may now be less acute. Being hugged can give them a sense of being loved that is very much what they need to know. Yet, often our only body contact with them is to take care of their needs — washing, bathing, lifting, dressing, shaving and hair combing.

Occasionally, an older person has an aversion to being touched. (I have yet to see or hear about an older person who does not respond to touching when it is finally used.) But if that is not the case, I strongly recommend that you hold hands with him or her. I have even had younger people tell me that holding their hands gives a strong sense of centering, helping them to concentrate. (If the person has arthritis, don't squeeze tightly. There is a difference between a firm hold and a tight hold. I like a firm handshake, but I don't like to have my hands squeezed until my rings cut my fingers!) Holding someone's hands can have the effect of bringing someone out of confusion into focus. Sit directly in front of the person, take both hands in yours and hold them firmly.

Verbal Responses

In my very first course in counseling, I learned a technique that has proved invaluable over the years. At first it seemed a little silly, and I felt foolish doing it. But over and over again, the value of this technique has been shown:

Repeat back word-for-word what was said to you.

If that sounds too silly, you can rephrase it into a question, *but use the same words* and repeat it back. Doing that serves two major purposes: *it lets the person talking know that you really heard them* and *it gives them an opportunity to clarify and add to the statement if they want.* Later on when you get more sophisticated in the use of this technique you can try paraphrasing what they said and repeat it back in slightly different words. But for now stick to repeating back exactly what they say to you.

Let's try it. I say to you:

> "I really don't like this applesauce."
> "You really don't like the applesauce?"
> "No, I don't. It's much too sweet."

"You don't like it because it's too sweet?"

"Right, and besides, it has too many raisins."

"You don't like it because it's too sweet and has too many raisins?"

So, now you have much more information on why I don't like the applesauce, and if anyone asked me, I'd say you were a tremendous listener!

Practice Pausing and Waiting

That conversation went pretty fast, but suppose there were a few pauses — times when I just didn't come right back at you. *Practice waiting.* Don't respond too soon. Some of us, and I'm one of the worst, are afraid of pauses, even short ones. If you're afraid of silence and keep talking to fill the gaps, you won't find out anything. Remember: The aged respond a little slower, sometimes a lot slower if there's been a stroke or some other debilitating loss, and they might need more time. You might want to try counting in your head and just see how long you can wait, all the while holding his or her hands and leaning forward attentively. Believe me, a mere 30 seconds can seem like an hour.

A note on leaning forward attentively. People have different space requirements. I don't like it when someone thinks they have to be nose to nose with me during a conversation; I like to have space between us. If someone is nearsighted, he or she won't be able to see as well if you're too close. Use your judgment and pull back if your listener responds to your nearness by leaning away from you. The same is true for eye contact and touch. The object is to make the elder comfortable and at ease with you. Use your best judgment.

Now let's try a conversation with a little more depth. I'll start:

"How is your son, Tim, doing?"

"He's not doing well at all."

"Tim is not doing well?"

"No, he's not." (Pause) "He has been doing very badly in school, and he's been staying out really late." (Pause) "He's been suspended twice and he may have to leave the school."

Now I'm getting to the problem.

Avoid Selective Deafness

One of the ways we fool people, and we get fooled, is by asking questions to which we really don't want the answers. Then we have to get ourselves off the hook by not listening to the answers that we didn't want to hear! Occasionally, someone needs to talk so badly they go ahead with all the answers you didn't want no matter how you turn them off by your poor listening techniques. More often, however, our non-listening cues are picked up quickly by such responses as, "Uh-huh," "What a shame" and "That's really too bad." Those responses are sometimes necessary because time is short or the location is purely social and doesn't call for long, in-depth interviews.

Respond Appropriately

Even on most social occasions, listening and responding appropriately will make you a very popular person. In fact, you probably won't get to the restroom all night! You might even be captured by one person and spend the whole evening listening to that person's woes. And if you should by any chance indicate that you have caregiving experience, watch out! You will be stuck in the corner with a beleaguered caregiver for the rest of the evening, and you will be begged for your phone number.

So, now you're attentively listening to Tim's mother's problems. You have repeated back what she has said, paused to wait for more information and kept eye contact. You have a feeling that you have all the information you're going to get. You are now ready for the next step. Respond to the *feeling* that is lying behind the words.

> "You're really worried about him, aren't you?"
> "Yes, I am. I don't know what I'll do if he's suspended."
> "You're feeling helpless."

"Yes, and I'm angry too. He acts like he doesn't even love me sometimes."

"You are angry [because you love him] and he's acting like he doesn't love you." (The brackets indicate an addition on the listener's part.)

"That's right. I love him so much, and I'm so afraid for him."

If you kept on like this you would soon have the whole story, feelings and facts. Not until then (and maybe not even then), would you begin to problem solve. But we're getting ahead of ourselves.

Focus and Be Patient

Now we'll try one that is harder and more appropriate for the subject matter of this book.

Remember: resist distractions and focus on the person; repeat what is said to you; practice waiting; respond to the feeling behind the words.

You are visiting your father in a nursing home. He is sitting in his chair, hunched over, head hanging down and looking at his hands as he moves them. As you come over and sit down in front of him you take his hands in yours.

"Hi, Dad."

"Hi, honey." (Pause) "Can I go home with you today?"

At this point, your own stomach will give a lurch, and you will feel guilty, sick, sad and generally horrible. But you're not going to respond from your *own* feelings, remember, but to *his* feelings. You're not going to explain for the hundredth time why he can't live with you. Or why you had to sell his home. You're going to respond:

"You want to go home with me today?"

"Yes, I really do. I don't like it here."

"You don't like it here?"

(Don't worry about sounding silly. He knows you're listening now.)

"I don't like it here. The food is not good."

(Don't get hooked into problem solving about seeing the cook, either. That may be appropriate some other time — but not now.)

"You don't like it here because the food isn't good?"

"No, the food is terrible. I like the food your mother cooked."

(The message is beginning to come through. Now you can use a little creativity in your response.)

"You miss mother's cooking."

"I sure do." (Pause) "I miss mother too."

(*That is the real message,* but hang in there even longer and you will strike a vein of gold.)

"You miss mom a lot."

"I really do. *I get very lonely here sometimes.*"

(There it is. The real message behind "I want to go home," and you were patient and attentive enough to find it.)

"*You're really feeling lonely today,* aren't you Dad?"

"Yeah, I sure miss you and the kids. How is Elizabeth doing in school anyway?"

"She is doing just fine. Do you remember when . . . "

And there you have it. Message coded and decoded and delivered. From there you can go on to talk about the family, ease the loneliness with the warmth of shared memories and maybe even go for a walk in the sunshine. Your father has the satisfaction of knowing that you heard his real message, that you didn't get angry with him just because you had heard that same old question for the 100th time. He may even stop asking it and, then again, he may not. But you have the decoder key now. Even if he uses a new statement next time, you can decode it.

No Reasons to Fail

I know what you're thinking: *That's great, but my problem is different. It won't work out so neatly. Dad has Alzheimer's or whatever.* I realize, as the author, I have the unfair advantage of being able to write it so that everything falls smoothly into place. Yet, even when I do it in person, it's surprising how often something unexpected and helpful comes up.

"I Don't Want to Be a Burden."

If this is a common refrain you hear from your parent, you really need active listening to find the real message. Let's listen in on a conversation between Samantha and Polly, her mother.

> "Hi, mom. How are you today?"
>
> "I'm just fine, Sam. You're late today."
>
> "I'm run ragged today. I just came to check on you and see if you're okay."
>
> "You don't need to do that, Sam. I don't want to be a burden."
>
> "You're not a burden, Mom. Have you been taking your meds?"
>
> "Of course."
>
> "Are you drinking your water? Look, your water cup is empty. You know you have to drink lots of water."
>
> "Yes, yes, I know."
>
> "Well, I have to get back home. Susie is sick this morning and I had to leave her alone to come here. I'll drop in later to see how you are doing. Bye."
>
> "You don't have to come again today. I'll be fine."
>
> "Later, Mom."

The words say "you are not a burden," but what is the *real* message here? If you were on the receiving end of Samantha's attention, what would your reaction be? I don't think I would be reassured that I was not a burden. The real message seems to be, "I've interrupted my busy schedule and my family to come here to make sure you are taking your medications and following orders." So how could Sam let her mom know that she cares about her and that, although she is a responsibility, she is not a "burden."

What if the conversation went something like this:

"Hi, Mom. Wait 'til I tell you what I saw this morning." (As Sam says this she is putting away some groceries in the cupboard.) "I picked up a few of the things you said you needed while I was doing my shopping this morning."

"Tell me what you saw."

"Well," Sam said as she sat down by her mom, "I saw a beautiful doe and her fawn on the side of the road. I thought of you and how you loved to see them in the spring and how you fed them in the winter. Do you remember?"

"Of course I do. They were so funny. The little ones jumped around and the big ones chased them."

"Yeah, that was great." (Pause) "Did you take your meds today?"

"Yep, every single one. That pill box you got for me really helps me remember."

"I know because I use mine every day, too."

(Looking around, Sam doesn't see her mother's water cup.)

"How about something to drink, Mom? Water? Tea?"

"I should probably have water. I think I forgot to drink it today."

"Water it is. I need some, too. It's really hot for this time of year. It's great to come and sit here with you in the air conditioning. So relaxing." (Sam sits down after getting the water, leaning back in her chair.)

"Don't you have someplace you have to be?"

"Soon, but not just yet. Susie's home from school with a cold so at home I'd just be trying to tune out her loud music anyway. Not too relaxing. Not like here." (Sam reaches over and takes her mother's hand.) "Did I ever tell you that I'm glad you're my mother?"

Her mom smiles. "Only every time you visit."

"Oh, sorry."

So what is the message now?

First of all, Sam's body language shows her comfort in being with her mother. Her words are not about what she is doing for her, but about something else, and the tasks assume a secondary importance.

There is a difference between a burden and a responsibility. Some days they feel the same. On those days it may be better to plan something other than visiting your parent. Often our true feelings come out in body language and attitude whether we want them to or not.

Don't give up.

Don't give yourself reasons to fail. Sometimes we make excuses for not doing something: "It won't work anyway" or "She doesn't pay attention to me" or "I'm not very good at this." We sabotage our own efforts by giving ourselves negative messages to excuse our failure to try something new.

Negative messages are destructive whether they come from someone else or from you. Your brain hears them all. You might try actively listening to yourself. Count the number of time you say things like, "That was stupid" or "How dumb can I be?" about yourself. Make an effort to use positive and affirming statements to yourself about yourself. Give yourself reasons to succeed, not fail. You can do it. You are smart, resourceful and determined. Go for it!

Let me reiterate what I have referred to in previous chapters: caring for an aging parent is the best motivation for making plans for your own old age. Looking into communities where you can be looked after when your own health fails is the best gift you can give to your own children and/or other relatives. If you don't want to be a burden, you must be deliberate in making sure it doesn't happen.

Trust the Process, and Practice

Have faith in yourself. Have faith in your ability to do what needs to be done. *And practice.* Find someone to practice on. Do it at the next social gathering you attend. That should be easy. Everyone wants to be listened to.

So, what do you think? Are you ready to try it? Why not? You have much to gain and little to lose by trying. If you're in constant or at least regular contact with your aged relative, then go ahead and give it a try. Wait until she makes some statement that looks promising and then just casually repeat it back to her. See what happens. Try it with one of your children, a spouse and a friend. Just do it.

And what about the touching? Does that scare you a little? Try it anyway. Be brave. Have faith. You might be surprised at the results. Don't be too tentative. Try to act confidently and just do it.

After you've tried putting into practice what you've learned in this chapter, be sure to record in your journal the reactions you got and how you felt about it. Then try it again and record it again. Pretty soon you can look back with wonder at how anxious you were the first time, and you'll have a record of your progress in black and white to prove to yourself that you can do it.

Beyond Listening

There is one time when listening skills won't do you one bit of good — that's when your relative doesn't talk.

I'm going through that right now with my mother, who gets tired (at 100, who wouldn't?) and sometimes she just doesn't want to talk. So lately I've started reading to her. And not a book that she might have read a few years ago but one I knew she would be able to focus on because she loves dogs and cats. The book is *Because of Winn-Dixie* by Kate DiCamillo. She loves it and brightens up immediately when I ask if she wants me to read.

Since my mother's mind is still active, my sister and my uncle sometimes do crossword puzzles with her, reading her the clues and the number of letters. They are always surprised at the extent of her vocabulary, even now at her advanced age.

The first elderly person I visited in a nursing home was of Swedish ancestry, and could speak that language, except that she had a stroke and could speak very little of anything. I began reading books about a Swedish girl growing up in America. The woman, who could barely speak, corrected my pronunciation whenever I came across a Swedish word in the text. And she corrected it without a hesitation of any kind.

Some guidelines about the books to choose:

- books heavy on action, low on description and explicit violence (typical young adult fiction);

- familiar titles and characters;

- books with childhood memories;

- books with historical or biographical themes that correspond to their age group (The Depression, World War II);

- books that are based on a hobby they might have (train stories, horse stories); and

- books that are set in their cultural or geographical neighborhood.

At age 100, my mother is often sleeping or at least not communicative when I visit. I am fortunate enough to have siblings who are retired, so, when I am available in the summer, we visit together. That way we can have a conversation and Mom can just listen. Occasionally she chimes in to let us know that she hears us, but mostly she lies in bed with her eyes closed, enjoying the sound of her children's voices. We always start by saying, "Hey, Mom, all your kids are here. Are you going to wake up and talk to us?"

She usually says yes but seldom actually wakes up much. Once in a while she corrects something we say or asks a question. During a recent visit, my sister, who was sitting near the foot of Mom's bed, murmured to my brother, who was sitting beside her, that she had just seen her doctor and she needed surgery. I was sitting near Mom's head speaking to her. Suddenly she turned to me and said, "What surgery? Why does Chris have to have surgery?" We were shocked. She is quite deaf but she heard that loud and clear. Of course, we reassured her that it was minor and nothing to worry about, but it impressed upon us that she does hear what we say, even if she doesn't have the energy to respond.

So, be inventive. Try listening if someone is talking, but if they are not speaking try something different. Don't be discouraged.

Exercise 6

Write out some responses you might use following the statements below — if you were really listening. See if you can re-create the verbal path to the real message in parentheses.

"I don't really want to go to this dinner tonight." (I feel old and unattractive.)

"Sometimes I get fed up with my brother." (I'm jealous because he can do no wrong in Mom's eyes.)

By the way, it's okay if your real message is different from the ones in parentheses above. Most of us will put our own messages into our examples. What does that tell you about me? Hard to keep secrets here!

Don't forget to keep writing in your journal. And keep practicing.

Chapter 7

What to Do When Values Collide.

Values

Where do our values come from?

For most of us the answer is diverse. Our first values are instilled in us by our families of origin. Some of us may have lived in three generational households where Grandma and/or Grampa came to live when they could no longer care for themselves. That gave us a feeling that it is the way care *ought* to be given. Sometimes it's a matter of unexpressed expectations. Our own parents, whether intentionally or not, may have given the impression that they expect to move in with us when and if it becomes necessary. With this intention making itself at home in our heads, it is hard to entertain any other solution when the time finally comes for action.

No matter how old we are, the thought of being a "good" daughter or a "good" son is always in the back of our minds. Preconceived ideas of what that means can block off avenues of behavior that might not fit the image.

Sometimes, however, the values we espouse are the result of our religious upbringing. The particular faith, its depth and sincerity may differ, but the built-in values are often similar. In some cases this limits the range of *caregiving options* open to us.

"My pastor says I'm doing the *right thing*. If I'm doing the *right* thing now, then if I later have to choose another option, is it the *wrong* thing? I am so confused."

This chapter attempts to ease some of the restrictions imposed on us by our value system, whether that system is grounded in our religion or simply based on cultural expectations. The following quotes are from the original *Leaders' Manual*, written for seminar leaders:

As we have worked with families, we have found that some people are imprisoned by incomplete theologies.

This is important because you need to know that we are not telling you your faith or values are wrong, or your pastor is wrong. Instead we are saying that these incomplete theologies may be *'incapable of inspiring the serious, hard-headed, persistent thought needed to cope with ongoing responsibility for an aging parent. Unexamined beliefs may even promote cultural expectations in the guise of commandments from the Almighty.'*

For example, we are told to *love* one another. But no one tells us *how* that works when one person's needs conflict with another's. How do we reconcile these opposing *loves?* And how about when our own needs are not being met? Are we not included in the loving system? Is it okay for one person to be *exploited* for the benefit of another?

Exploitation

Let's talk about exploitation for a minute.

There are times when we put aside our own needs for someone else. We do it for our children. We do it for other members of our immediate family. Usually we do it for the short term. Our children grow up. Others get well or learn to care for themselves. But what about those times when the situation calls for long term care, a putting off of everyone else's needs, including your own, in the service of one person. Those times call for more serious thought.

Sacrifice versus Exploitation

It seems to me that for a sacrifice to be a true sacrifice, rather than exploitation, it needs to have three basic characteristics:

1. sacrifice is *voluntary*, not forced;

2. sacrifice is something that *needs* to be done, not just what someone *wants* you to do;

3. sacrifice must be something *only you* can do, something that cannot easily be done by others.

Your Relationship

In the long run, the only thing you can offer your parent is your relationship. If you use up your patience and energy on chores that could be done as well — or even better — by someone else, then you will not have the resources left for your unique relationship with your care receiver.

When I first started visiting a woman in the nursing home, I read to her, and we talked about the books we read. Sometimes, if her meal was served while I was there, I helped feed her.

One day she put up her hand and stopped the fork halfway to her mouth. In her stumbling, stroke-slowed voice, she said, "You are not for that!"

She wanted me for companionship, not for services the staff could perform. In her wisdom, she knew that feeding her was not something I was required to do; others could do it.

One woman in our seminar, we'll call her Joyce, visited her mother every day in the nursing home. Every day her mother verbally assaulted her, blaming her daughter for her own unhappiness. Finally Joyce figured out an assertive response: she said to her mother, "Obviously you aren't feeling good enough for visitors today. I'll come back tomorrow. Maybe you'll feel better then," at which point she turned and walked out. Knowing Joyce could and would leave caused her mother to exert some self control and she began changing her behavior.

Guidance

A word about *guidance*. Whether one believes the guidance we receive comes from God, from a higher power or from our own inner resources, guidance doesn't operate well if we don't pay attention to it. You know the phenomenon: "I keep telling my teenager not to text while driving, but does he listen? No!" So, when he runs into a tree while texting, can he blame his mother for not telling him about the tree?

That's how some folks treat guidance. They just refuse to accept it because it doesn't fit their own ideas of what should be done. Then they blame God or someone else when things don't work out. Or they look for wisdom to fall from Heaven instead of recognizing it when it comes from the lips of a neighbor.

One of our seminar participants, we'll call her Anne, was struggling with a dying parent and with Jake, her out-of-control teenager. At one of our meetings Anne mentioned the problems she was having with Jake to another participant.

The other woman said, "I know of a boarding school that would be perfect for Jake."

After much discussion Anne called the school, set up a visit and subsequently enrolled her son, thus freeing herself to help her mom with her dying father.

Two years later her son graduated top of his class.

Maybe God spoke directly to Moses on the mountain, but often *we* hear the voice of *guidance* in the experiences of our fellow human beings.

So, what do you think?

Are you ready to do some of the *"serious, hard-headed, persistent"* thinking necessary to clarify your values? Okay, here goes.

Exercise 7

Make a list of everything you are doing for your aging parent, from laundry to driving to the doctor, to cooking, dressing — everything. Line them up neatly so you can write next to them.

Now go back over this chapter and examine each task in light of the following criteria:

- Are you doing it *voluntarily?* Are you a *cheerful giver?*
- Is it truly *necessary?*
- Are you the *only one* who can do it?

If the answer to one or more of these questions is a resounding, "No!" then you might want to rethink your behavior. Maybe what you thought was loving sacrifice is actually the result of lifelong domination and approval-seeking, which often leads to exploitation.

If you ask for guidance, *be prepared to be changed.* It took two years for Joyce to stand up to her mother. It changed their relationship in significant ways. Instead of one accusing and the other defending her actions, they now spend time talking about family members and reminiscing about more satisfying times.

Remember this: *"Caregiving is a journey; it can turn out to be a pilgrimage."* *

---

*   The quotations in this chapter are from *Help for Families of the Aging (Leaders' Manual)* by me and Jane Dewey Heald and are used because they were so well written to begin with that I can't do better, even now! And, of course, they are used by permission of the authors.

Chapter 8

What Next? Is There Light at the End of the Tunnel?

So you've read this book. You've done the exercises and asked yourself the questions at the end of each chapter. Maybe you've carried this book in your handbag or in your briefcase, on airplanes and in doctors' offices. It is underlined and re-underlined and now the binding is going. And things have improved. But you look ahead and see a long haul. There are no short, easy fixes. It is still hard.

Is there something more you can do? Something to help you get through the hard times, the frustration, the guilt and anger, the sorrow and pain?

Maybe so. This chapter holds suggestions for possible future action. There is nothing here you *must* do. You may *want* to do more. We'll begin with the easiest action.

Reading

Reading about your situation is about the easiest response. Choose something from "Appendix B: Suggested Reading" that might hold some information of help to someone in your circumstances or go online and check out what is available. Amazon has many titles of interest to a caregiver, but if you don't want to buy them, you can make a note of the titles and authors and check them out at your local library.

Sharing

Perhaps you are ready to share what is going on in your life with a friend, a pastor, a social worker or a therapist. If this person is not a professional in the field, make sure they read "Appendix C: Notes to the Listener."

At this time you may not have the energy or time to do more than the above, but if you do, there are two more options to think about.

Discussion Group

Many books now have discussion questions at the end of the actual text. These are to be used for getting book group discussions off to a start. Appendix D: Group Discussion Questions lists questions focused on caregiving issues and some larger issues as well. Certainly you could start a discussion group based on this book or another caregiving book.

Support Group

It takes time, energy and high motivation to begin and carry out support group functions. We have found that parental caregivers are often drained of these resources and thus cannot begin a support group. When their caregiving duties are over, most want to move on, away from the pain of the past. They are not equipped to carry on the long term agenda of an ongoing support group.

However, if the energy is available to you, or if there is a pastor or friend who can help, the remainder of this chapter is a how-to guide for starting and maintaining a support group for caregivers.

How to Begin

In the process of reading this book, I hope you have found at least one other person with whom you can share your thoughts and feelings. Maybe it's someone in your church or synagogue, maybe in your PTA, maybe someone you met at the park when he/she saw you reading this book. If so, that's great because when you start your group meetings, you will need a co-leader, someone to share ideas and responsibilities.

Meeting Times

Scheduling is important. Because some caregivers are home bound it's a good idea to have evening or weekend meeting times when other family members may be at home to take over caregiving duties. However, *the most important people are you and your co-leader.* Schedule meetings at a time that is convenient for you. If others want to be there badly enough they'll figure out a way. Desperate caregivers will find the time and energy to come and be willing to change. Do keep in mind that a support group is not an educational seminar, although it can have educational components. This is a sharing, caring group, and folks who are not willing to share, or who are judgmental, will hold people back from their greatest growth. At the end of this chapter, I list the affirmations to be read at the beginning of each meeting. These will set the philosophy for the group.

Meeting Place

Although a church or synagogue seems a logical place, it actually doesn't work too well. Members of those congregations may feel inhibited about exposing themselves as desperate caregivers. Running into friends who inquire about the group may be embarrassing. A better choice is a bank meeting room, a community center, a school or a library. Our local supermarket has such a meeting room.

Start Small

Start with an announcement in your church bulletin, a brochure on the library bulletin board, a letter to the social workers at local nursing homes and assisted living centers. We put brochures in hair salons and talked to hair dressers, even bartenders, folks who hear lots of personal stories from their patrons.

What To Do During Your First Meeting

Actually, this is probably what you will do on each subsequent meeting because new people will come and others will drop out. You need to assume that each meeting group is new and knows nothing.

Each leader reads a prepared paragraph about why they are starting this group and what they hope it will accomplish. It might read something like this: "My name is Carol, and I am here because I read a book, *The Best You Can Do*, which helped me to be more loving to my mother, who is in a care center." Your co-leader might say: "My name is Sally, and I'm here because I take care of Mom in my home, and it is getting more and more difficult. I need the support of other caregivers to get through this."

You then pass around a sheet of affirmations. Each person reads one aloud as it gets to him/her, who in turn passes it on until all are read. The leader can then say, "If you stay, we assume you are willing to abide by these affirmations, especially the first one about non-judgment and confidentiality." The first one is the cornerstone of any support group. The affirmations provide the philosophy of the group. If anyone feels they should not be there, this is the time for them to leave. The suggested list can be found in "Appendix A: Affirmations."

Go around the room asking them to identify themselves by first name and tell their caregiving situation: "My name is Jane and my mother-in-law has Alzheimer's and is living with me and my husband."

> **Key:** No one is to comment on the situations. No one says, "You're just like me" or "How could you put her there?" — or anything. The leader says "Thank you," and moves on to the next person until all who want to share have done so.

After my first seminar, a professional therapist asked me how I got people to share their stories. I told him that sharing wasn't the problem.

The problem was to get them to *stop* sharing. Because of this need to be heard, I suggest beginning each meeting with small-group sharing. You can break into groups of two, three or more. However, if there are more than two people in a group, someone must time them (an egg timer works nicely). If there are three people and they have 30 minutes before returning to the main group, then each person can tell his/her story for only 10 minutes. Timing is important because, sometimes, once a caregiver has a sympathetic ear, there is no stopping them. If they break into dyads (twos) the leader needs to keep the timer.

Before they break into their small groups, go over the rules for good listening:

- *Listen, don't speak.*
- *Be attentive, resist distractions. Do not offer suggestions, judgments or criticisms.*
- *Lean forward. Nod your head to show that you understand.*
- *When the person's time is up, thank them but don't comment further.*
- *Touch only if it seems appropriate.*

After the sharing time might be a good time for a break. It gives folks the option to keep sharing or stop for a while. Decide ahead of time if it will be a timed respite or a refreshment break. Food can make complications, and some venues don't like food in their meeting rooms. Make the break long enough for restroom visits and water fountain stops. Then resume. Five, ten minutes tops.

Once back in the large group, outline your plans for the next three months, telling them there will always be a sharing time. This will be more and more important as they know each other better. Before leaving, they may want to exchange phone numbers or plan one-on-one meetings outside of the group meeting.

End the meeting with a reading, maybe from *The Best You Can Do* or another caregiving book.

You may find that it is occasionally appropriate to feature a knowledgeable outside speaker who will be helpful to members of the group. I suggest a sharing time first, a break and then the speaker. Give the speaker a topic and a time period. The idea of having the speaker on last is to prevent the whole meeting to be taken up with someone else's ideas. The members need to share their stories and if they don't do it at the beginning of the meeting, in twos or threes, they will interrupt the speaker to get their stories told.

Another idea for a program is to take one of the affirmations and open it to discussion after the break. You may even want to ask each member to buy *The Best You Can Do* and go through it, chapter by chapter, in the second half of the meeting. The first half should *always* be for sharing. "Appendix D: Group Discussion Questions" can also provide topics for this period.

Watch out for long-winders who never get enough air time. If this is a continued problem, appoint a time-keeper so that each person is timed for 2–3 minutes, at which point the timer bell goes off. (Use the old fashioned wind up timer, not an electronic one. The bell is louder and it only rings once so it doesn't drive everyone crazy. I have one that looks like a lady bug so I can joke about cutting people off. "This lady bug is such a tyrant, always wanting her own way!")

Do not give out the leaders' phone numbers. Participants can exchange numbers with other members who agree to be called, but you as leader do not want middle-of-the-night phone calls from desperate caregivers. It's important to limit your involvement to the meeting. *This is not an AA group for which folks are encouraged to take calls at all times of the day or night.* As a caregiver yourself, you do not have the time or energy to be on the end of numerous crisis calls. Your first responsibility is to take care of yourself. Remember, it's permissible for you to do whatever it takes to keep your sanity.

Caregiver support groups are different from support groups that support people as they recover from addictions. It is not unusual in the latter groups to find members who have been coming for ten, twenty, even thirty years and more. Caregivers, on the other hand, often quit attending the groups once their situation changes due to a death or some other event. *And that's okay!* It may be hard for other members to understand that sometimes caregiving is so painful that, once it's over, reminders are not welcome. This is another good discussion point for the group to tackle after their break.

Before I speak or lead a group, I spend some time in prayer or meditation, clearing my thoughts and gathering my spiritual energy. If I know the group, I envision each member of the group, hoping that what I say will connect with at least one person. You cannot solve anyone else's problems, but sometimes your message can provide relief for a troubled soul. That is why I wrote this book. It has been a labor of love, love for all of you who, like me and my family, are doing the best you can do for yourself and your aging parent.

Exercise #8

Whether simple or complex, it helps to list your next steps in order of what you want to do. You might make a list like the one below.

1. Check Amazon.com books.
2. Call my pastor for an appointment.
3. Put a notice in the church bulletin asking folks who might be interested in a discussion group on this topic to call me.
4. Make time in my schedule for a walk in the park every day.

Just do it!

Figure 4: The Adjustment Process

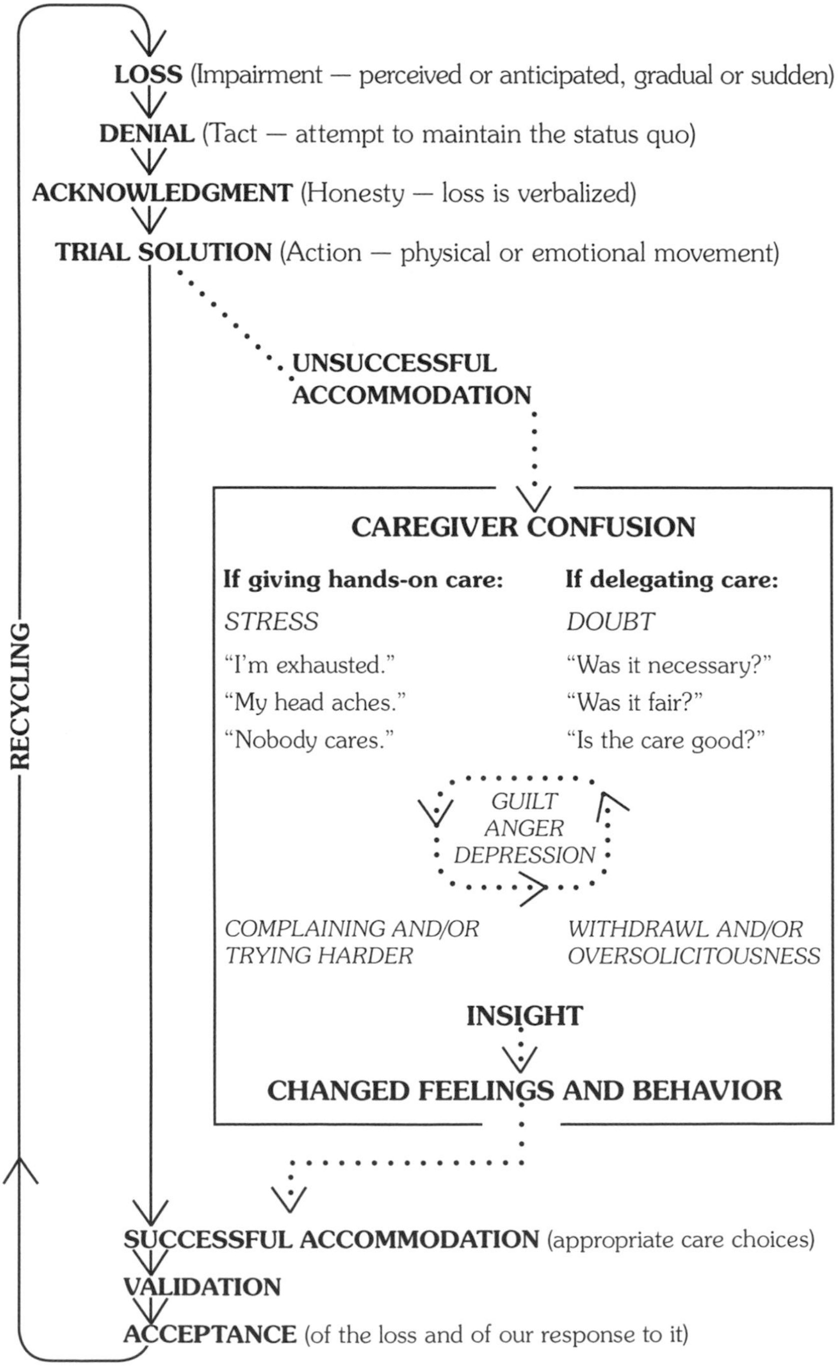

LOSS (Impairment — perceived or anticipated, gradual or sudden)

DENIAL (Tact — attempt to maintain the status quo)

ACKNOWLEDGMENT (Honesty — loss is verbalized)

TRIAL SOLUTION (Action — physical or emotional movement)

UNSUCCESSFUL ACCOMMODATION

RECYCLING

CAREGIVER CONFUSION

If giving hands-on care:	**If delegating care:**
STRESS	*DOUBT*
"I'm exhausted."	"Was it necessary?"
"My head aches."	"Was it fair?"
"Nobody cares."	"Is the care good?"

GUILT
ANGER
DEPRESSION

COMPLAINING AND/OR TRYING HARDER   *WITHDRAWL AND/OR OVERSOLICITOUSNESS*

INSIGHT

CHANGED FEELINGS AND BEHAVIOR

SUCCESSFUL ACCOMMODATION (appropriate care choices)

VALIDATION

ACCEPTANCE (of the loss and of our response to it)

Chapter 9

From Quicksand to Solid Ground.

During my work with the aged and their families, I identified a process that many (but not all) individuals and/or families go through when a parent needs help. (See Figure 4 for a diagram of the process.)

The Adjustment Process

Let's go back to Chapter I and use Joan for our first example. Obviously, losses occurred that forced Joan's family to recognize that her mother needed help, that she couldn't live alone. Maybe she wasn't eating well and didn't want to cook. Maybe she had quit taking care of her personal hygiene. They probably spent some time denying that any of those were the case; but, eventually, the loss was acknowledged, verbalized, and Joan's mother came to live with her.

Looking at the chart, you can see that I call this a *trial solution.* It's always a good thing to try something before committing yourself to it for the foreseeable future. However, Joan didn't do that. She could have asked her mom to stay with her for a month or longer, leaving the future open ended so her mother could return home later. Very few of us have the necessary foresight to choose that option. Sometimes we rush in, sell our parent's home, burning our bridges as we go. Burning bridges is not a good idea.

So Joan ended up in the area of the chart that I call *unsuccessful accommodation*. And she was stuck there in the "quicksand." Her journal records her negative feelings, the result of this inappropriate action.

So what if, at some point, Joan chooses the assisted living option, moves her mother to a small apartment where she can have her meals provided, home care for any necessary nursing, and emergency response should she need it. Sounds ideal, doesn't it? But often the parent is unhappy with this solution and lets everyone know it. Then doubts creep in: Was that action really necessary? Could I have kept her at home if I just tried harder? Wouldn't she be happier with us? It wasn't perfect, but we could have done it.

Excuses, Excuses

Sometimes families who use the nursing home option find themselves withdrawing from their parent, visiting less and less often, finding more and more excuses *not* to visit. This is understandable. We are pain-averse people. If we visit Mom every *three* days and feel sick and/ or guilty for the next two days, then it makes sense that if we only visit once a week, we will still feel guilty for two days — but it is only two-sevenths of our week, not every day. Sometimes the pain is so bad that we just quit visiting, abandoning our elder to avoid the hurting.

Conversely, some families visit regularly, not missing a single day. They don't take vacations or visit grandchildren, using the excuse of having to visit Dad. This may *sound* good; but, in fact, it is not necessarily good. Visiting *every* day doesn't allow the parent to adjust to his surroundings and learn to rely on the staff for help. Dependence on his children can actually increase beyond what it needs to be.

The Search for Validation

Whatever action a caregiver takes, the feelings of guilt, anger and depression can color the caregiver's entire life, giving them a feeling of being trapped in the emotional quicksand of caregiving.

What can the beleaguered caregiver do? Unfortunately, there are no perfect solutions. With people living longer, sometimes unhealthier, the best we can do is try to find a solution that causes the least pain and discomfort to all parties. You notice I didn't say *no* pain and discomfort, just *the least*.

Occasionally, everything works out almost perfectly. Mom and/or Dad are relatively happy in their new situation and the caregiver(s) can live with it as well. That is called *successful accommodation* on the chart. It is often *validated* by the care receiver, who makes statements about how happy they are in the new apartment or how great it is not having to cook.

More often, the validation has to come from within the caregiver or from other family members. When my mother had to be moved from my sister's home to a nursing home because it was impossible for my sister to care for her adequately, it was her daughter, my brother and I who shored up her resolve, telling her over and over again, "You can't take care of her anymore." Her daughter, an LPN, put it more succinctly: "Mom, she is a two-person assist now and you are one person." More than that, it would have meant that two people always had to be in the house together, an impossibility in their situation.

The fact that someone we love is too old to live on their own or outside of an institution is a hard one to accept. It helps when the older person realizes the inevitability of the action. That is the best validation one can have.

Successful accommodation leads to acceptance of the losses and sorrow that may accompany it . . . until the next loss occurs and a new accommodation must be found. It is a process, one which doesn't end until a parent dies. Even then, the sadness and guilt hangs around, making life uncomfortable for a long time.

A Look at Guilt

There are people who think guilt is a positive feeling, that it keeps us motivated to do the *right thing*. I don't agree with that. Guilt is often unreasonable, an expectation that we *should* have done something we couldn't actually do. Rather than motivating us to do the *right* thing, it often comes *after* an action, one we usually cannot do anything about. Guilt is a spoiler, coloring our lives with its dis-ease.

It is our conscience, our sense of values, that motivates us to search for the right answers in situations that are difficult. This is our *inner compass*. It points us in the right direction just as a geographic compass points north. How does the decision make you feel? Loving? Burdened? Peaceful? Agitated? All these feelings are indications given to us by our core values, our inner compass.

It is following our compass that gives us peace in the long run. Guilt will always be with us, no matter how hard we try to avoid it. And there will always be regrets when the parent is gone, actions we wish we had or hadn't taken. After three weeks of being with my father night and day while he was dying, I thought of one little thing I had neglected and was in agonies about it. I have heard this same story from other family members. Guilt is not open to reason, and it will always find something on which to feed.

Because of that, it doesn't pay to say to yourself, "I must do it this way so I won't feel guilt when my parent is gone." You will feel guilt anyway because guilt is an irrational feeling. Your inner compass should be your guide because it is based on your core values.

Did you do the best you could do? That, after all, is the most anyone can expect of you, including yourself.

Exercise #9

Where are you in the chart? Near the beginning? In the middle with roiling guilt upsetting your stomach? Feeling peaceful and at ease with yourself? Make a list of your feelings now, right at this moment, to help you find out where you are in the process. Remember, it is a *process*, one that recycles, so you can be in more than one stage at the same time. It's okay. You're on the right track. Just hang in there. I'm cheering for you.

Epilogue

Epilogues are one of my favorite book divisions. Sometimes I just can't bear to leave the wonderful characters behind, and I want the added information about their lives. I have been known to read a book multiple times because the characters are such good friends.

I hope you feel like that about this book. Maybe you *bonded* with certain people whose stories touched your heart. Maybe one or two caused a switch to be flipped in your head and you have taken courageous action as a result.

All the examples are based on real people or on composites made up of real people — people who have struggled as you are struggling. By the time you read this there will be an e-mail address so you can write to me and tell me your story, hopefully a success story.

I wrote this book because I care about **you.** I want you to fulfill your obligations while enjoying your life. It sounds easy, but it is not. It takes hard work and hard-headed thinking. It is not a simple process. But you can do it. You have the resources within you, and I have faith in you. So, go for it!

Here is my hope and prayer for you:

May you find the power within you to grow and change;
May your responsibilities rest lightly on your shoulders;
May you have the support of loving family and friends;
May your life be filled with blessings.

Appendix A

Affirmations

1. We accept each other without judgment and are willing to offer and receive mutual caring and support in total confidentiality.

2. We are receptive to new skills and insights.

3. We are open to learning new ways of relating to the elderly.

4. We expect change as part of life; people can learn to understand and handle change.

5. We realize that we cannot control all the circumstances of our lives or of our loved ones' lives; we *can* work on our own reactions to them.

6. We believe that each person in our family — including ourselves — is entitled to a fair share of our time and resources.

7. We help each other consider alternatives, acknowledging that we can be more loving to our aging relatives when we are comfortable with our level of involvement in their care.

8. We summon courage to look at the reasons for any compulsive behavior that is giving us trouble.

9. We do not base our decisions on the approval of others.

10. We admit that we cannot produce happiness for anyone else, including our aging loved ones, neither can we expect to fill all their needs.

11. We strive to clarify what is important to us and to consider any decisions on the basis of our true values, recognizing that any decision involves a cost.

12. We search for meaning in our experience and seek to appreciate the benefits of knowing our relatives in their old age.

Appendix B

Suggested Reading

Your local librarian can help you discover new and well-reviewed books and other resources on the topic of caregiving and aging parents. Many librarians are available online to help you — even after hours. If you don't know how to use a computer, a research librarian can help you at your local bricks-and-mortar library. It is a great resource, and, of course, checking out books is *free*. If your library doesn't carry a specific book, ask about Interlibrary Loan from another library.

Below are a few of my favorite recommendations:

Books

The 36-Hour Day: A Family Guide to Caring for Persons with Alzheimer's Disease, Related Dementia Illnesses, and Memory Loss in Later Life by Nancy L. Mace and Peter V. Rabins, M.D. (A classic in the field)

Man's Search for Meaning by Viktor E. Frankl

What Do I Do? How to Care for, Comfort, and Commune with Your Nursing Home Elder by Katherine L. Karr

When Love Gets Tough: The Nursing Home Decision by Doug Manning

Online

If you type in "aging parents" or "elder care" or "senior care" in the search box of your online browser, you will find many helpful sites. Try to stick with sites that are associations or organizations and not those with "snake oil" to sell you.

Most states have many resources for the elderly (and their caregivers). Start at your state's website and search for a department for the elderly (see "Appendix D: States' Websites on Aging"). Be aware that different states may use different terms, such as elders, seniors, aged, etc. Three good resources are listed below:

Organizations

Alzheimer's Association (http://www.alz.org) Offers state chapters, a Helpline, support groups, online resources, education programs, a huge library, safety services, fundraisers, and, most importantly, their online Community Resource Finder, which provides instant access to community resources and services. To learn more about all they have to offer, visit their "About Us" page.

Children of Aging Parents (http://www.caps4caregivers.org) A mission to assist caregivers of the elderly or chronically ill with reliable information, referrals and support, and more.

Eldercare Locator (http://www.eldercare.gov) A public service of the U.S. Administration on Aging that can connect you to services for older adults and their families. They can also be reached by telephone at 1-800-677-1116.

Appendix C

Notes to the Listener*

Listening is a skill; we can *learn* a skill. Although it is true that some people seem to be natural listeners and do it better than others, there is no magic to it. In the next pages you'll get some pointers on how to let people know you are really listening to them.

Body Language

Since our bodies speak, use yours to speak for you. Sit facing the person you are listening to, maintain comfortable eye contact and lean forward in an attentive attitude. (Note: In some cultures eye contact is disrespectful. Do what is comfortable for you and your partner. If you are in doubt about it, just ask him or her.) Resist distractions. Focus on the person.

Verbal Responses

In my very first course in counseling, I learned a technique that has proved invaluable over the years: *Active Listening*. At first it seemed a

---

* From Chapter 6

little silly, and I felt foolish doing it. But over and over again, the value of this technique has been shown. *Repeat back word for word what was said to you.* If that sounds too silly, you can rephrase it into a question, *but use the same words* and repeat it back.

Using the same words serves two major purposes: *it lets the person talking know that you really heard them and it gives them an opportunity to clarify and add to the statement if they want to.* Later on, when you get more sophisticated in the use of this technique, you can try paraphrasing what they said and repeat it back in slightly different words. But for now stick to repeating back exactly what they say to you.

Let's try it:

I say to you, "I really don't like this applesauce."
You reply, "You really don't like the applesauce."
I say, "No, I don't. It's much too sweet."
You say, "You don't like it because it's too sweet."
I add, "Right, and besides, it has too many raisins."
You affirm with, "You don't like it because it's too sweet and has too many raisins."

So now you have much more information on why I don't like the applesauce, and if anyone asked me, I'd say you were a tremendous listener!

How to Wait and Respect Personal Space

That conversation went pretty fast, but suppose there were a few pauses — times when I just didn't come right back at you. *Practice waiting.* Don't respond too soon. Some of us, and I'm one of the worst, are afraid of pauses, even short ones. If you're afraid of the silence and keep talking to fill the gaps, you won't find out anything. You might want to try counting in your head and just see how long you can wait. Believe me, a mere 30 seconds can seem like an hour.

A note on leaning forward attentively: people have different space requirements. For example, I don't like it when someone thinks they have to be nose to nose with me during a conversation. Pull back if your listener responds to your nearness by leaning away from you. The same is true for eye contact. The object is to make the other person comfortable and at ease with you. Use your best judgment.

Now let's try a conversation with a little more depth:

You say, "How is your son, Tim, doing?"

Tim's mother answers, "He's not doing well at all."

You repeat her words: "Tim is not doing well?"

"No, he's not." She agrees, then pauses and adds, "He has been doing very badly in school and he's been staying out really late." (Pause.) "He's been suspended twice and he may have to leave the school."

Now You're getting to the problem, and you've given Tim's mother the time to let you know what's going on with Tim.

Don't Fool Around

One of the ways that we fool people and that we get fooled is by asking questions to which we really don't want the answers. Then we have to get ourselves off the hook by not listening to the answers that we didn't want to hear! Occasionally, someone needs to talk so badly that they go ahead with all the answers you didn't want no matter how you turn them off by your poor listening techniques. More often, however, our non-listening cues are picked up quickly by our uttering such vacant responses as "Uh-huh," "What a shame" or "That's really too bad." These responses are sometimes necessary because time is short or the location is purely social and doesn't call for long, in-depth interviews.

Even on most social occasions, though, listening and responding appropriately will make you a very popular person. In fact, you probably won't get to the restroom all night! You might even be captured by one person and spend the whole evening listening to that person's woes. And if you should by any chance indicate that you have caregiving experience, watch out! You will be stuck in the corner with a beleaguered caregiver for the rest of the evening and begged for your phone number.

Respond to the Feeling

So now you're attentively listening to Tim's mother's problems. You have repeated back what she has said, paused to wait for more information, and kept eye contact. You have a feeling that you have all the information you're going to get. You are now ready for the next step. Respond to the *feeling* that is lying behind the words.

"You're really worried about him, aren't you?" You ask, sincerely.

"Yes, I am. I don't know what I'll do if he's suspended."

"You're feeling helpless," you say, picking up on her feelings.

"Yes, and I'm angry too. He acts like he doesn't even love me sometimes."

"You are angry [because you love him] and he's acting like he doesn't love you." (The brackets indicate an addition on the listener's part.)

"That's right. I love him so much and I'm so afraid for him."

If you kept on like this you would soon have the whole story, feelings and facts.

Remember: resist distractions and focus on the person; repeat what is said to you; practice waiting; respond to the feeling behind the words.

Now you are ready to listen to your friend or fellow support group member. Keep practicing. Good listeners are always in demand.

Appendix D

States' Websites on Aging

The website URLs listed below were current at the time of this book's publication. Some URLs are quite long, such as the one for Colorado, and difficult to key in. If you find that the links are too difficult to key in or the one shown does not work, use the search feature on your internet browser and search for: state of [name the state] aging.

Many of the sites below feature a way to narrow down resource information by county and even by city.

Canada is listed at the end, for the convenience of our northern readers.

If you are unfamiliar with how to search or access internet sites, ask your local librarian for assistance.

Alabama (http://www.caregiverlist.com/Alabama/
departmentonaging.aspx) Department on Aging and Elder Services

Alaska (http://www.alaskaaging.org/) Department of Health and Social Services, Alaska Commission on Aging

Arizona (http://www.azgovernor.gov/aging/) Department of Economic Security, Division of Aging and Adult Services

Arkansas (http://www.daas.ar.gov/) Department of Human Services, Division of Aging and Adult Services

California (http://aging.ca.gov) Department of Aging

Colorado (http://www.colorado.gov/cs/Satellite/CDHS-VetDis/CBON/1251595238465) Department of Human Services, Aging & Adult

Connecticut (http://www.ct.gov/AGINGSERVICES/site/default.asp) Department of Social Services, Aging Services Division, State Unit on Aging

Delaware (http://www.dhss.delaware.gov/dsaapd/) Division of Services for Aging and Adults with Physical Disabilities

Florida (http://elderaffairs.state.fl.us/index.php) Department of Elder Affairs

Georgia (http://aging.dhs.georgia.gov/) Department of Human Services, Division of Aging Services

Hawai'i (http://www.hawaiiadrc.org/) Aging and Disability Resource Center

Idaho (http://www.idahoaging.com/) Commission on Aging

Illinois (http://www.state.il.us/aging/) Department on Aging

Indiana (http://www.in.gov/fssa/2329.htm) Family & Social Services Administration, Division of Aging

Iowa (http://www.aging.iowa.gov/) Department on Aging

Kansas (http://www.kdads.ks.gov/) Department for Aging and Disability Services

Kentucky (http://chfs.ky.gov/dail/programs.htm) Cabinet for Health and Family Services, Department for Aging and Independent Living

Louisiana (http://new.dhh.louisiana.gov/index.cfm/subhome/12/n/7) Department of Health & Hospitals, Office of Aging & Adult Services

Maine (http://www.maine.gov/dhhs/oads/aging/resource/aaa.htm) Department of Health and Human Services, Aging & Disability Services

Maryland (http://www.aging.maryland.gov/) Department of Aging

Massachusetts (http://www.mass.gov/dph/healthyaging) Health and Human Services, Healthy Aging and Disability Unit

Michigan (http://www.michigan.gov/miseniors) Office of Services to the Aging

Minnesota (www.dhs.state.mn.us/aging/) Department of Human Services, Aging

Mississippi (http://www.mdhs.state.ms.us/aas.html) Department of Human Services, Division of Aging & Adult Services

Missouri (http://health.mo.gov/index.php) Department of health & Senior Services

Montana (http://www.dphhs.mt.gov/sltc/index.shtml) Department of Public Health & Human Services, Senior and Long Term Care

Nebraska (http://dhhs.ne.gov/medicaid/Pages/ags_agsindex.aspx)
State Unit on Aging

Nevada (http://aging.state.nv.us/) Department of Health and Human
Services, Aging & Disability Services Division

New Hampshire (http://www.dhhs.nh.gov/dcbcs/beas/aging/index.
htm) Department of Health and Human Services, State Committee on
Aging

New Jersey (http://www.state.nj.us/health/senior/index.shtml)
Department of Health, Division of Aging Services

New Mexico (http://www.nmaging.state.nm.us/) Aging & Long-
Term Serices Department

New York (http://www.aging.ny.gov/) New York State Office for the
Aging

North Carolina (http://www.ncdhhs.gov/aging/) Division of Aging
and Adult Services

North Dakota (http://www.nd.gov/dhs/services/adultsaging/)
Department of Human Services, Adults and Aging Services

Ohio (http://aging.ohio.gov/home/) Department of Aging

Oklahoma (http://www.okdhs.org/divisionsoffices/visd/asd/sca/)
Department of Human Services, Aging Services Division

Oregon (http://cms.oregon.gov/DHS/spwpd/Pages/offices.aspx)
Seniors and People with Physical Disabilities

Pennsylvania (http://www.aging.state.pa.us/portal/server.pt/
community/department_of_aging_home/18206) Department of Aging

Rhode Island (http://www.dea.ri.gov/) Department of Human Services, Division of Elderly Affairs

South Carolina (http://aging.sc.gov/Pages/default.aspx) Lieutenant Governor's Office on Aging

South Dakota (http://dss.sd.gov/elderlyservices/index.asp) Department of Social Services, Adult Services & Aging

Tennessee (http://www.tn.gov/comaging/) Commission on Aging and Disability

Texas (http://www.dads.state.tx.us/) Department of Aging and Disability Services

Utah (http://www.hsdaas.utah.gov/) Department of Human Services, Aging and Adult Services

Vermont (http://dail.vermont.gov/) Agency of Human Services, Department of Disabilities, Aging & Independent Living

Virginia (http://www.vda.virginia.gov/) Department for Aging and Rehabilitative Services, Virginia Division for the Aging

Washington (http://www.aasa.dshs.wa.gov/) Aging & Disability Services Administration

West Virginia (http://www.wvseniorservices.gov/) Bureau of Senior Services

Wisconsin (http://www.dhs.wisconsin.gov/aging/) Department of Health Services, Services for the Elderly

Wyoming (http://www.health.wyo.gov/aging/index.html) Department of Health, Aging Division

Canada (http://www.phac-aspc.gc.ca/seniors-aines/index-eng.php)
Public Health Agency of Canada, Aging & Seniors

Appendix E

Group Discussion Questions

The following questions can be wrestled with in small groups or in the large group:

1. Are people who are old or ill entitled to more consideration than people who are healthy? Why?

2. Affirmation #10 (p. 80) states: "We admit that we cannot produce happiness for anyone else, including our aging loved ones, neither can we expect to fill all their needs." To what extent do you agree?

3. When you become old, what kind of relationships do you want? With your children? With your spouse? With your friends? Think in terms of dependence and independence.

4. How important is it to you to be liked by everyone? Is it hard for you to disagree with people?

5. How is responsibility for an infirm spouse the same as or different from responsibility for an infirm parent?

6. Is it helpful to try to fulfill your *spouse's* responsibility for his/her parent? When does taking over caregiving duties for your spouse actually deny them the benefits of the relationship?

7. Do you think it is possible to hide feelings of frustration, anger or resentment from a care receiver? If not, how do you think they feel when sensing a caregiver's negative feelings. What is a good way to handle these negative feelings?

8. If we never got along with a parent in the past, how can we expect to change the situation when they become dependent?

9. When a parent refuses to accept help and insists on living in an unsafe environment, what actions can a caregiver take? When is it too soon to take control? Can you just walk away when they become stubborn and refuse help?

10. What does it mean to be comfortable with a situation? Does it mean you like it? Does it mean you are at peace with it?

About the Author

Carol Spargo Pierskalla, Ph.D.

Carol Spargo Pierskalla, wife, mother of three, and teacher of adolescent girls, changed the direction of her career after a hospital encounter. In her own words, "One year I spent my Christmas vacation days in a hospital for diagnostic tests. My roommate was a seventy-five-year-old woman, a victim of stroke. Even though she had limited speaking ability, we became friends and when I returned home I followed up, finding her in the local Presbyterian nursing facility. For the next several years, I called on her regularly, read to her, and was inspired by her to move from teaching adolescents to working with elderly."

Pierskalla enrolled in the counseling psychology graduate program at Northwestern University in Evanston, Illinois and graduated with a Ph.D. and a specialty in gerontology, the study of aging. Over the next years she had the opportunity to launch the National Support Center for Families of the Aging. From this organization came the Seminar for Families of the Aging, which morphed into *The Best You Can Do: For Yourself and Your Aging Parent.*

Although Dr. Pierskalla enjoys older people and is a caregiver herself (her mother turned 100 in 2012) her special concern has been and continues to be the families of the elderly. "Caring for a parent in our society is definitely a challenge," Pierskalla says. "Our mobility, our independent life styles and generational differences can cause real hardships when parents become ill or disabled in some way."

She sees *The Best You Can Do* as an outreach to all the struggling families who are trying to do the "best" they can for their aging parent(s). Visit Dr. Pierskalla's website at www.CarolPierskalla.com.

The author, Carol Spargo Pierskalla, Ph.D. with her 99-year-old mother, Annie Alfreda Schrader Spargo, in September of 2012. (Photo by Image Photography)